FAILING FAMILIES, FAILING SCIENCE

Failing Families, Failing Science

Work-Family Conflict in Academic Science

Elaine Howard Ecklund and Anne E. Lincoln

NEW YORK UNIVERSITY PRESS
New York

NEW YORK UNIVERSITY PRESS
New York
www.nyupress.org

Library of Congress Cataloging-in-Publication Data
Names: Ecklund, Elaine Howard, author.
Title: Failing families, failing science : work-family conflict in academic science / Elaine Howard Ecklund and Anne E. Lincoln.
Description: New York : New York University Press, 2016. |
Includes bibliographical references and index.
Identifiers: LCCN 2016010267| ISBN 978-1-4798-4312-1 (cl : alk. paper) |
ISBN 978-1-4798-4313-8 (pb : alk. paper)
Subjects: LCSH: Scientists. | Scientists—Family relationships. | Work and family. |
Science—Vocational guidance. | Science—Study and teaching (Higher)
Classification: LCC Q147 .E336 2016 | DDC 306.3/6—dc23
LC record available at https://lccn.loc.gov/2016010267

New York University Press books are printed on acid-free paper, and their binding materials are chosen for strength and durability. We strive to use environmentally responsible suppliers and materials to the greatest extent possible in publishing our books.

Manufactured in the United States of America

10 9 8 7 6 5 4 3 2 1

Also available as an ebook

CONTENTS

ACKNOWLEDGMENTS

We are thankful to the undergraduates, graduate students, and post-doctoral fellows who tirelessly collected and analyzed data as part of the Perceptions of Women in Academic Science study. Special thanks to Catalina Crespo, Jon Endean, Katherine Sorrell, Meagan Alley, Meghan Binford, Sarah James, and Vineeta Kapahi. Many thanks to undergraduate and graduate students who helped with data analysis: special thanks to Esther Chan, Claire Cummins, Celina Davila, Douglas DeVries, Hasitha Dharmasiri, Darian Dolenc, Allison Ecklund, George Enriquez, Naomi Fa-Kaji, Alyssa Fornara, Katie Fusco, Daniel Gillespie, Molly Goldstein, Mauri Gustafson, Henry Hancock, Jessie Ho, Cecilia Hutchings, Leigh Anne Jackson, Patrick Kelly, Rachel LaTouche, David Liou, Alley Lyles, Ryan Mulvenna, Laura Orr, William Pahl, Kelsey Pedersen, Rija Qureshi, Sara Smith, Cassandra Tansey, Kseniia Tokarieva, Ann-Hunter Van Kirk, Virginia White, and Lilly Yu. Thanks to Susan Ecklund, Laura Achenbaum, Heather Wax, Hayley Hemstreet, and Shelby Allen for manuscript preparation help. Thanks to Gwynn Thomas of the University at Buffalo, who read the manuscript in its early stages. This book was reviewed as part of the Religion and Public Life Program's Books in Public Scholarship workshop. We are grateful to Erin Cech, Melinda Fagan, Sally Gallagher, David Johnson, Xavia Karner, Mary Ellen Konieczny, Laura Kramer, Elizabeth Long, Kirstin Matthews, Maria Oden, and Jared Peifer for taking the time to review this work in its entirety. Any weaknesses are ours alone.

Thanks to the National Science Foundation, Gender in Science and Engineering Program, for generously funding this research through grant number 0920837. We're thankful to New York University Press and our editor Ilene Kalish. Finally, we extend our gratitude to our families. Elaine is especially grateful for the support of Karl and Anika.

1

When Nothing Matters Except Science

> The main discrimination in the sciences I see is this idea that there is an ideal scientist. There's one particular type of person who does science. They like to work fourteen-hour days, and they think in a particular way, and their one and only passion is doing research. . . . I'm not that person, [and I] wonder if that means I'll never be a good scientist.
> —Jennifer, physics graduate student[1]

Jennifer, a twenty-five-year-old physics student, fell in love with science while she was in high school, after she read *Cosmos* by the astronomer Carl Sagan. She has spent years pursuing her academic studies, and she is doing well in her graduate program. Yet she is questioning her future in academic science—how well she can fit in, her ability to succeed, whether she will be able to have a family and be a successful scientist, and whether she has what it takes to be good at the career she thought she wanted.

When we met her, Jennifer, one of the most professionally dressed and articulate scientists we interviewed for our study, wore jeans and a blue blazer, accessorized with a nice scarf. We were surprised to learn her young age and that—although it seems she is just starting—she is already questioning her future in science. Jennifer also exemplifies a sea change in academic science. She is troubled by her perception that there is an unspoken expectation to be "an ideal scientist," and as a result, she questions her own ability to succeed in science even though she is doing well in her graduate program.

That is because, for quite some time and still today, science has promoted a strong and clear idea of the "ideal" scientist, and it doesn't match up to someone like Jennifer. An "ideal type," according to sociologist Max Weber, is the central form of a group or an idea that we all treat as if it were true, whether or not it is.[2] The ideal type becomes the expectation that insiders seek to live up to and that outsiders expect. From listening to scientists, we learn that the ideal scientist in the American university is a man, with a supportive wife who takes care of all his personal matters. If his wife is employed, her job takes a backseat to his; his scientific work is seen as a "calling"; her work is seen as "just a job." This ideal scientist knew from a very young age that he wanted to do science and was always encouraged and inspired by his family. He never had any doubts about his desire to pursue this career. The ideal scientist often starts out as a lonely graduate student who spends most of his time on work, with few outside interests and little yearning to pursue other activities. As an established scientist, he has cultivated an ability to overcome any obstacles to getting work done. His work takes priority over family life. The ideal scientist can have children and often does, but his scientific work receives his full and undivided devotion. Work is his joy, his hobby—his whole life.

There are still some scientists who live up to this ideal, or are trying to. Most cannot. On these pages, we argue that they *should* not. The nature of science is changing, and, with it, so must the model of the ideal scientist and the structure of science itself.

Who Is the Ideal Scientist?

Arthur is a professor in his early seventies who leads a bustling physics lab where he started as a postdoctoral fellow decades ago. Still bearing a felt-board office directory that looks straight out of the 1970s, Arthur's lab building harkens back to a different time—and, in many ways, Arthur does too. He describes himself as "arrogantly confident." When asked how he balanced work responsibilities with being a father to his two now-grown sons, he explained that, over the course of his fifty-year marriage, his wife "did everything . . . I did physics and she did the rest." Echoing Arthur's sentiments, another senior professor of physics, in his early sixties with two grown sons, admitted, "I like working, it's basically my hobby. It's wonderful that people would pay me to do what I'm doing . . . don't tell anyone, but I would do it anyway if given the opportunity!"[3]

For these men, science is much more than a profession. It is their lifestyle, their passion, their ultimate pursuit, and the core of their identity.

These men represent the ideal scientist. They also represent a minority of the scientists we studied. Yet the ideal version of what it means to be a scientist remains fixed. This presents a problem.

Sociologists argue that "professional role confidence—individuals' confidence in their ability to successfully fulfill the roles, competencies, and identity features of a profession"—is a central personality feature of those who persist in science.[4] So now we must answer a number of questions. Are scientists like Arthur the typical case? Not anymore. Are scientists still expected to live up to the ideal that Arthur embodies? We think they are. Is the university structure set up to prefer and facilitate the success of scientists like Arthur, men who have wives managing all spheres outside of their husbands' scientific work? We believe it is. And this brings us to the crux of the problem: the "ideal" type is nearly impossible for the majority of today's academic scientists to attain and maintain, and as a result, many are unable to achieve the all-important professional role confidence. This is true for *both* men and women. Young men in science today are more like Jennifer than Arthur. And Jennifer is more than just one individual. Jennifer will likely be a casualty of an academic science that is not just unappealing to young people but unmanageable and unsustainable for those already pursuing it. Here we provide the individual stories and reasons for those like Jennifer, whose experiences are deeply embedded in and birthed from an academic science structure that is at risk because it refuses to recognize that work and family life are now deeply interconnected for both men and women in science. As a result, many young scientists will choose to leave academia altogether, and as a result science will suffer.

The Nature of Academic Science

In 1998, sociologist of science Joseph Hermanowicz described academic science this way:

> Elite departments provide ample resources and rewards for excellence in research, the sole criterion for evaluating professional and personal worth. Elite scientists hold themselves and each other to uncompromising standards, severely sanctioning those who do not continually produce acclaimed research. Success only ratchets expectations higher, and one

> derives status solely from one's most recent work. Thus, perhaps surprisingly, although they are most successful in terms of research, elites fear professional failure more than other scientists do. They also suffer more from this fear, because science looms large in their overall self-identities.[5]

Researchers find that men in professional occupations have strong devotions to the world of paid work.[6] Among middle-class men, such commitment demands long hours and a strong identification with career, which is often expressed as an all-consuming commitment to their employer.[7] The ideal academic scientist is devoted to his research, which affords him a type of "macho" masculinity that is linked to long hours spent at work.[8] Among elite professionals, long hours are even seen as a badge of courage, signaling a primary commitment to the workforce[9]—and academics average longer hours than most professionals.[10] For example, previous work on academic scientists at elite research universities (which our data confirm) reveals that both men and women work upwards of fifty-five hours a week.[11] These extremely high expectations for scientists are tied to the idea that science is concerned with ultimate truth, and thus obviously worthwhile, with long hours justified because they signal a meaningful pursuit of this truth.[12] Consequently, academic science is seen as a "greedy institution" that often claims a person's full temporal and cognitive attention.[13]

In recent years, academic science has become even more demanding of the total person. In times past, scientists—especially those at major research universities—needed less funding, so they did not experience the frenetic pace of grant writing, management, and fund-raising that we see today.[14] Their relationship with the public has changed as well. With easily accessible information that appears scientific, the public thinks it knows more about science than ever before, which means that scientists are pushed by the public and by the science infrastructure itself to do more science outreach. And federal agencies are now calling for more social application of science, meaning that even the most basic research (research done only to pursue scientific knowledge without any specific societal application in mind) must be rationalized to the public as "helping society." In addition to doing cutting-edge research, scientists must now engage in outreach programs that show how their science serves society.[15] There is less affirmation of basic research for its own sake.

All these factors mean that successful scientists at major research universities now often manage multi-million-dollar-per-year research enterprises, which involve getting grants, being concerned about retaining full-time lab employees whose jobs are dependent on their grants, doing public outreach as a condition of getting and keeping grants, and serving on granting committees. All this is alongside teaching undergraduates, mentoring graduate students and postdoctoral fellows, serving on university committees, and remaining active members of professional networks and associations necessary for getting tenure. There are fewer university jobs, less affirmation of novel ideas, and greater pressures to get tenure-track jobs—and the even greater pressures of keeping these jobs after they are landed.

Another big change is the increasing number of women who are entering careers in academic science. This has led to new areas of work-family conflict. Because science is a time-demanding profession that allows for few responsibilities and commitments outside of work,[16] and because family responsibilities generally tend to fall on women more than men,[17] gender norms and disparities are directly linked to work-family conflict for women in academic science.[18]

What is interesting, however, is that we are also seeing greater work-family conflict for men in academic science. More and more, male scientists have wives and partners who are part of the paid labor force, and the expectations of the ideal scientist often conflict with the ideals of modern fatherhood. Today, men feel compelled to be their family's primary breadwinner while also being highly involved with their children—what psychologist Kerstin Aumann and colleagues, who study broader societal changes related to family life, call the "new male mystique."[19] They claim that men are pressured to "do it all in order to have it all," in a way that is similar to the pressures felt by women in the workforce.

One research study found that in 1965, fathers reported 42 hours of paid work per week, compared with 37 hours in 2011, while their hours spent on housework increased from 4 to 10. In 1965, men reported spending an average of 2.5 hours per week on child care, while in 2011 they reported spending 7 hours per week. (Child care hours for mothers also increased from 10 to 14 hours per week.)[20] Another study found that 95 percent of men would like to spend more time with their families.[21]

With more women entering science, and more men in science actively participating in housework and child care, the population of elite scientists is significantly different and more diverse than it used to be.[22] *We argue that these changes are good for the structure of science; more diversity among scientists means more diverse and better science.* Yet, while the demographic makeup of academic science is shifting dramatically, the institution of science is not. It is still suited to an earlier generation of scientist—a man with a stay-at-home wife.

Despite dramatic changes in the labor force and family structure over the past fifty years, society generally still sees separate spheres for husbands and wives: wives care for household activities, and husbands act as breadwinners for their families.[23] Child care is still believed to be more the responsibility of women than men.[24] Based on these traditional views, academic institutions still expect that male scientists will fully devote themselves to work without the burden of household chores or family obligations. In reality, however, many male scientists are now part of dual-career couples, and they must balance their work lives with their personal lives—managing their households, maintaining their relationships, and caring for their children. And academic scientists routinely face more limited job prospects when they are married to another scientist.[25]

What is unique about academic science is that perhaps more than some other professional fields the model of academic science is based on the ideal scientist. At the structural level science has not fully changed to accommodate family life at the same rate as other professional spheres. This means there are fewer male scientists who can pursue science all the time and anytime. In other words, there are fewer and fewer ideal scientists.

Why Does It Matter?

Reaching the level of tenured faculty, the pinnacle of achievement in academia, is a more momentous task than it has ever been. Four years of undergraduate studies are followed by four to six (or more) years of PhD work. By the time a scientist earns her doctorate, she is likely to be in her late twenties, the time in the life course when most Americans are beginning to settle down. Scientists still must undertake at least one, and increasingly multiple, postdoctoral appointments, which usually range from two to six years, and because many postdoctoral positions are dependent on grant funding, they do not offer the competitive pay, benefits, or stability of private sector jobs.

Next comes an appointment as an assistant professor, lasting five to seven years, and finally (if successful!) a tenured associate professor appointment. At this point, most scientists are in their late thirties or early forties, well past the time most Americans have started raising children. The time as a tenure-track professor is perhaps the most intense and stressful in an academic life, with no specific timeline for moving from associate to full professor. In this highly competitive and lengthy process, when is the right time to start a family? Scientists in academia often feel they have to wait until they are tenured, a perception that has led to a trend of later childbearing among scientists.

Even in the best-case scenario—once they manage to secure a job, earn tenure, and start a family—academic scientists still must deal with the heavy demands of their career, which often impinges on time set aside for family. The academic science workday has no strict boundaries, and academic scientists feel a constant pressure to produce more publications and earn more grants and awards. They also worry that prioritizing family obligations could have negative ramifications for their careers. Concerns over how to balance work and family are not eased at the most elite research universities, which supposedly provide the most resources to support their employees and are leaders in their organizational field.[26]

The inability to balance life as a scientist with life as a parent is more than a personal issue or a female issue. It is a structural failure resulting from the expectation that the ideal scientist will prioritize complete and utter devotion to career above all else.[27] While the fixed view of the ideal scientist has real consequences when it comes to gender equality—much research suggests that fully qualified women leave science at higher rates than do men—we find that the fixed view of the ideal scientist has a significant impact on the ability of *both* women and men to stay in and succeed in academic science.

Research shows that academic scientists who are mothers pay the highest price. A 2010 study found that married women with children are 27 percent less likely than married men with children to achieve tenure in the sciences, and 13 percent less likely to earn tenure than are married women without children.[28] One likely explanation for this effect is an underlying assumption that being a mother distracts from or compromises a woman's devotion to her work.[29] What happens as a result? Numerous women we spoke with indicated that they actually felt it necessary to "hide" their children until after receiving tenure.

And yet we found that male scientists also say that issues related to family can have a great impact on their academic careers. While many of the men we interviewed felt privileged to be more involved in their children's lives than were past generations of male scientists, many of those who are parents noted that their family commitments often negatively affect their opportunities for career advancement. Because they want to spend more time with their children, they are unable to devote as much time to their research as are their childless peers. They say senior male scientists subtly and overtly sanction them for devoting themselves too much to their families—for example, criticizing them for not being fully devoted to their work when they take time off after the birth of a child.

The tensions men feel between work and home are multiplied when their partner or spouse also works in a professional career, which is increasingly the case for male scientists today.[30] When faced with the same work-life challenges that women face (such as marriage to a spouse in a full-time profession or lack of adequate child care), some men curtail their careers as much as their female counterparts. Single and childless scientists also suffer under the expectations of the ideal scientist. They feel that their desire to take care of family matters and pursue any interests outside of work is often not validated.

The feeling that career progress has been hindered by the difficulty of balancing work and family has a negative effect on satisfaction as a faculty member (and it is safe to assume that faculty satisfaction is linked with retention and productivity). Our research also shows that even though there are pronounced differences between male and female scientists in their satisfaction with work, we find no gender difference in their happiness with life outside of work when controlling for other factors.[31] Once we add an intriguing variable—desired number of children—we find something fascinating: male faculty who have fewer children than they desired are less satisfied with their lives than are the women in our study, even though female scientists tend to have fewer children than their male colleagues and are less likely to have children at all. Clearly, neither sex can be ignored in the push to expand the family-friendliness of academic science.

When surveyed, one in four graduate students and one in five post-doctoral fellows said they were considering a career outside science altogether, and those who said that they have fewer children than they want because of their science career are much more likely to desire a career outside science. In our interviews with scientists, they said over and over again that the difficulties they have with maintaining family commitments will play a particularly important role as they decide whether or not to stay in academic science.

Economist Albert O. Hirschman's organizational theory of exit, voice, and loyalty provides some insight into why many scientists struggling to balance work and family end up leaving academia.[32] He explains that members of an institution will remain loyal to an institution when they disagree with its policies *if* the organization provides them with the opportunity to bring change. Interviews with biologists and physicists reveal their perception that universities and departments are unwilling to change to support those who do not live up to their fixed notion of the scientific ideal.

This is a book about how women *and* men who are scientists at the top U.S. research universities negotiate their personal and family lives and how the strategies they use *and the identities they develop* have the potential to change the actual structure of academic science by moving it beyond the image of the ideal scientist—the scientist who pursues science as a calling at the cost of everything else. Elite academic science has changed and become much more accommodating to women, leading to an increase in the number of women in most disciplines in science, although women have still not reached parity with men. *Yet we argue that while women are hit harder by the pressures of elite academic science, the institution of science—and academic science, in particular—is not good for either women or men who want to have children or pursuits outside of their careers.* Our research reveals that women still experience difficulty "having it all," and—perhaps most important—both young men and young women scientists struggle with balancing their work and family lives. This struggle may prevent these young scientists from pursuing positions at top research universities, a cost that is too great for our national science infrastructure to bear.[33] We argue that science itself is better off if it can accommodate those in different life situations. We stand alongside theorists of organizational and institutional health who argue that when organizations that rely on creativity for success (as academic science does) are more diverse, this leads to better and more robust creative output. At its core, the image of the ideal scientist is an issue because it reproduces gender inequality, strains families and children, and makes academic science an unattractive career choice for the best and brightest (who often have families as well), all factors that are structurally hurting science itself. These findings ought to be of concern to scientists, university leaders, policy experts, and members of the broader public who want the United States to continue to be a leader in world science.

How Did We Come to These Conclusions?

The data in this book are drawn from the Perceptions of Women in Academic Science (PWAS) study, which we led. When this research began, we planned to tell the story of how scientists perceive *women's* achievements in science and impediments to achievement for women in science. As research often does, ours uncovered something we were not expecting. While women definitely discussed discrimination in science, we were surprised to find that *both women and men* mostly talked with us about work-family dynamics in science. This is the story we present here, largely in their own words. Because certain voices seemed to capture the essence of what entire groups are thinking, the narrative is structured around a few scientists, like Jennifer, who embody the major findings and themes revealed by the larger study.

The PWAS study includes two parts: a quantitative survey of 3,455 scientists in biology and physics, which received a response rate of 72 percent (a very high rate in modern-day survey research),[34] and 150 interviews with biologists and physicists at the universities surveyed. In this way, we paint a full picture of the lives of academic scientists—combining the breadth that comes from surveying a large number of people with the depth that comes from follow-up face-to-face discussions. (More information about the details of our study can be found in appendix A at the end of the book.) Although we wrote this book together, we conducted different aspects of the research, and so from here on out, we will sometimes refer to ourselves separately, as Elaine and Anne.

We surveyed biologists and physicists at the top twenty American universities in late 2008 and early 2009 and then followed up between 2009 and 2011 with in-depth interviews with a random sample of those who responded to the survey. Most of the interviews were conducted in person by Elaine. The list we put together of all scientists in five career stages (graduate student, postdoctoral fellow, and assistant, associate, and full professors) at these universities included more than 14,000 individuals at thirty-one universities and 100 departments. We then randomly selected scientists from among these twenty graduate programs to participate. Elite Research 1 universities, a rank given by the Carnegie Classification of Institutions of Higher Education, were selected because these institutions largely shape what is seen as ideal in a given field. Scientists in the disciplines of biology and physics were selected for several reasons. First, the number of women in biology is increasing at all stages of the academic career path, while the number of women in physics remains very low.[35] At American colleges and universities, women constitute 46 percent of the life science faculty but only 14 percent of physics faculty. In the related discipline of astronomy, 19 percent of faculty members are female.[36] One possible reason for this, as some scholars have recently argued, is that physics is a discipline that people believe requires superior innate talent or brilliance, and such fields are likely to be dominated by men.[37] Second, we wanted to know whether biology, a discipline that now has as many women faculty as men, would be friendlier to family issues. We found that the cultures of these two disciplines are extraordinarily different.[38]

We also chose to survey and interview both senior and junior scientists. Senior scientists at top institutions most actively mold their disciplines, transmit scientific knowledge to the next generation, and broadly influence the practice and perception of science across sectors.[39] Junior scientists (graduate students and postdoctoral fellows) in the top graduate programs are on a path to becoming leaders in their fields and professors to the next generation of scientists.[40] Senior scientists are key informants on the structure of science, as well as potential agents of change. Junior scientists are the future. Only by surveying and interviewing both groups could we truly and deeply understand the role professional and personal expectations play in scientists' lives throughout the career course, and how changing work-life dynamics are shaping academic science as a whole.

We spoke with graduate students and postdoctoral fellows about their professional and personal aspirations—their thoughts about entering academic science, as well as the struggles they face in trying to obtain an academic science position while starting a family. We spoke with those who have "made it" in science by obtaining positions as professors, asking them about the hardships they face as they try to balance devotion to work and family, and what kinds of strategies they use to overcome the difficulties. We also examined their potential to change the institutional infrastructure of science. Through our interviews, we were able to dig into some deeper issues. To what extent are the long hours academic scientists devote to work a matter of individual choice? How much are they determined by larger institutional structures? Just how gendered are the difficulties associated with being simultaneously a parent and a scientist? Do these difficulties affect women more than men? Is the structure of university science itself gendered, or is science neutral when it comes to how to raise a family and have a career as a leading scientist? What makes the university science environment unique when it comes to examining the family-work tensions faced by all those in professional careers?

This work is also personal. Elaine's husband is an academic scientist, and together they have encountered the difficulties that come with trying to balance their relationship and careers. They have also faced the difficulties that come with balancing an academic science career and raising a young child. Their daughter was born during the course of data collection for this book. As Elaine was interviewing scientists about their lives and how they manage personal and professional responsibilities and commitments, she often brought along her baby daughter and found she was navigating many of the same issues they shared with her. As the child of mathematics teachers, Anne became interested in science at an early age. Her acceptance to the North Carolina School of Science and Mathematics, a public residential high school that emphasizes those subjects, further cemented a lifelong love of science and exploration. After initially majoring in animal science in college, Anne turned instead to the study of people, though her interest in science persisted. She studied the feminization of the veterinary medical profession for her dissertation and has studied science careers extensively with Elaine.

Book at a Glance

In *Failing Families, Failing Science*, we look at how gender, choice, and institutional structure shape science careers, and how science careers, in turn, shape family life. Our research reveals that *both* female and male scientists find structural barriers in the university setting that restrict their ability to raise a family and have a life outside of work, and this drives significant numbers of academic scientists to the corporate world or into other careers outside of science, where they believe a balance between work and family is more feasible.[41]

In the next chapter, "Family Matters to Science," we look at the degree to which elite scientists today feel they are living up to their image of the ideal scientist and the ways in which they try to integrate family life with their scientific work. We also explore the various ways that family life is important to science and the U.S. science infrastructure. In chapter 3, "Will I Make It? Family Life for Young Scientists," we hear from graduate students and postdoctoral fellows who tell us that finding a faculty position in science is not necessarily their goal, even though they have devoted many years to training for such a post. For many of these scientists, a strong desire to be near family or have a family takes precedence over an academic career, and they feel jobs in industry may provide more flexibility and be better able to meet their needs and wants, especially if they are in a relationship with another professional or academic.[42] "I want to read to my kids every night, and I don't want to quit my job, I would go crazy," says Christine, a biology postdoctoral fellow in her early thirties.[43] "I could never be a stay-at-home mom all the time, but I want to be able to be there for soccer games and reading and homework." Concerned that an academic lifestyle would "just be too hectic," she is considering a career outside of academic science—notwithstanding the almost ten years of postgraduate study she has devoted to biology.

In chapter 4, "Managing the Controlled Crash," we show that although graduate students and postdoctoral fellows may believe that their careers will stabilize and accommodate their families once they earn tenure, the experiences of senior scientists suggest that work-family struggles continue long after the tenure clock stops ticking. Carolyn, a full professor of biology who is married to another scientist at a major research university, is by all accounts a success story, but we quickly learn just how much she had to sacrifice to get there.[44]

Often, male scientists see their female colleagues as not fully belonging in the academy, though we found this sentiment to be stronger in physics than in biology. We also found that when these women have children, it seems to confirm male beliefs about their lack of professional dedication. As a result, the women we talked with disproportionately discussed the impact their science careers had on family planning, such as deciding when to have children, how many children to have, or whether to have children at all. In chapter 5, "When the Ideal Scientist Meets the Ideal Mother," we show that female scientists, as a whole, hold different beliefs than male scientists do about the contributions women *ought* to make to family life. In addition, men and women frame their contributions to family life differently. Men describe their family contributions as sacrifices, whereas women emphasize how "lucky" they are if their partner contributes equally to child-rearing tasks. Even though men are responding to new pressures to be involved parents, adopting strategies for work-family balance that have previously been used by women, the self-descriptions illustrate that the mental and emotional pressures are greater for scientist mothers, who are trying to simultaneously fulfill the obligations of two full-time roles.

Finally, in chapter 6, "A Way Forward for Universities, Science, and Scientists," we argue that universities must restructure their science departments to better meet the needs of the modern academic scientist, or they risk losing both women and men (though the failure of academic departments to account for and address gender differences and responsibilities outside the workplace could keep them from attracting more women specifically). We challenge universities and departments to implement structural changes that better accommodate the personal lives of modern scientists, and we encourage them to take a more active role in teaching young male and female scientists how best to balance their careers with family responsibilities through mentoring, classes, and workshops. After hearing the stories of those we have interviewed, we also encourage today's young scientists to develop personal strategies that allow them to succeed in academic science while having the kind of family life they want.

When it comes to balancing work and family, scientists deal with the same kind of struggles as everyone else. Yet they also deal with a professional ideal that is nearly impossible for them to live up to if they have a working spouse or any interests or commitments outside of work. The "greedy institution" of academic science is uniquely challenging and demanding. The perception that academic science is an especially inhospitable place for those desiring children and involvement in family life should be important to us all. We trust our top universities to generate the best and brightest scientists, to keep our country at the forefront of scientific knowledge and research, and to address the most pressing problems of our time. It is a national problem if the family-unfriendliness of academic science is a turnoff for the most talented men and women. We want the best scientists in the best universities doing the best research.

Ultimately, this is a book about change—the changing nature of academic science, the changing priorities of academic scientists, and the institutional changes that U.S. research universities can and need to make to retain scientists like Jennifer. As we have begun to see, the struggle to balance academic science and family life is not just a woman's problem. The large majority of scientists today—both male and female—are not willing to pursue science at the cost of everything else. The ideal scientist is a thing of the past, and it is time to leave this faulty image behind. The future, as they say, is now.

2

Family Matters to Science

So, my husband's moving . . . tomorrow to go live in DC. I will stay [here] for however long it takes . . . it's the path that a professor has to take, which is grad school and then the postdoc and probably a second postdoc, and then finally maybe you get an offer to be a professor, and hopefully you get tenure . . . there's a lot of moving around. And when you're looking for two jobs, that's difficult. . . . We don't want to . . . start having kids until we're definitely living in the same city.
—Jackie, graduate student in physics[1]

If you're going the academic route then you have to get tenure and you have that seven-year period after you finish your postdoc. So by the time you're done with that, you're forty years old already, or something like that. If you're planning on going into any other sort of nonprofit world, into industry, it's not going to be near as much [of] a problem.
—Kyle, graduate student in biology[2]

Family and Science as Linked Institutions?

Families are generally the first place that scientists develop a love for science. Many scientists we met shared stories about parents who were particularly supportive and encouraging of their academic pursuits—whether the parent was a high-level scientist or an individual without a college degree. For many an early interest in science—stoked by their families—led them to a career they adore. An associate professor of biology in her early forties told us how much she was influenced by time spent with her dad, a medical researcher:

> When I was young I would hang out in his office in the lab and meet the people, and we had people stay at the house, so I knew the people as cool and interesting people, and that my dad got to travel a lot and the family got to travel a lot. And those were also sort of intriguing things career-wise—that it would expose me to interesting people and interesting places.[3]

Many scientists have parents who are scientists. Among the scientists we studied, about 20 percent had one parent—generally the father—who is a scientist or engineer. Early socialization into science appears to be critical when it comes to pursuing a science career. A thirty-three-year-old assistant professor of biology, whose father was a physicist, joked that she has to "blame—blame [*questioning tone*]" her parents for her decision to pursue science.[4] She believes that "through interacting with them, I understood what being a scientist is about," and this was a critical complement to her formal education because it gave her insight into the reality of an academic lifestyle.

Jackie, the promising physics graduate student in her late twenties who is quoted in an epigraph to this chapter, recalled her father's influence on her decision to become an astronomer.[5] From a young age, she said, "Dad was very insistent on me being a computer scientist or an engineer," encouraging her to pursue "technical fields" because he believed these offered viable career options. Today Jackie recognizes that she felt his influence and recalls showing the most interest and promise in technical fields as a child, which she attributes to her father.

But Jackie, we found out, has already changed her scientific field in the hope that it will help her and her husband find academic jobs in the same city, and she anticipates many more challenges on the horizon. She fears she will not have a future in academic science. Christine, a postdoctoral fellow in biology, has lost hope altogether.[6] Despite devoting more than ten years to her discipline, she recently decided to leave academic science because of its family-unfriendly culture and the feeling that she will be unable to bring any real change in this regard. She will soon become one of the many women who leaves science prior to achieving a tenure-track position.[7]

Kyle, the other graduate student quoted in an epigraph to this chapter, worries about his ability to have a family as a scientist; as a result, he plans to leave academia after finishing his PhD. Another young male biologist told us that, to accommodate the demands of his wife's graduate studies and care for his two small children, he has made a commitment to working less than he would otherwise, and his ability to gain tenure may be at risk as a result.[8] Even though they are just beginning their careers, these young scientists are already acutely aware of how a commitment to academic science could affect their family life.

More established scientists in tenure-track positions confirm the fears of these young academics. They tell us that the difficulties of balancing work and family plague the entire career course. When Hilary was being evaluated for promotion and tenure, she hid the fact that she had children in order to guard against "motherhood discrimination."[9] Joanne, an assistant professor of biology who has a two-month-old son, has suffered from discrimination by her male colleagues; she said, "You don't want to be too much of a mommy kind of person in this career."[10] We will get to know each of these scientists better throughout these pages and will see just how closely family life is related to a career in academic science.

It is important to note that we will be using a broad definition of "family" here. When the prominent social scientific journal of family studies *Journal of Marriage and Family* changed its name by removing "the" in front of the word "family," the editors argued that "the" suggested there is only one form of family, rather than multiple variations. Scholars agree that families come in various forms and are not necessarily related through blood kinship.[11] In this book, we use "family" to refer not only to heterosexual parents with biological children but also to same-sex parent couples, adoptive parents, those caring for elderly parents, and other extended family connections. That said, when they use the term "family," most of the scientists in our study are referring to heterosexual marriages and biological children.

Decades of research emphasize the many ways in which work and family are inextricably linked: satisfaction with work, satisfaction with family and leisure, and the work-family nexus.[12] We extend this research more fully to scientists. We go so far as to call family and academic science "linked institutions." Thinking of work and family as linked institutions leads us to explore the empirical relationships between these institutions and examine the ways in which their norms, ideals, expectations, experiences, and perceptions anchor and influence one another.[13]

In many high-status professions, it is common for work to interfere with family life, and for family life to interfere with work, explains sociologist Scott Schieman and his colleagues.[14] But we argue that in science, the tension is worse, stemming from a specific but common framing of science as the "ultimate objective truth."[15] Consequently, doing science becomes a kind of *moral* rather than just a time commitment, the sort of activity that is worth putting everything else on hold to pursue. If science is perceived by scientists to be the fundamental source of truth, then a career in science is the highest calling, and other callings—like having a family—rightfully need to fall by the wayside.[16]

For example, one full professor of biology, who is married to a high school librarian and is the father of a seventeen-year-old girl and a twelve-year-old boy, told us he feels he is as productive in his research as he wants to be and experiences no constraints on his time.[17] He admits that having children has detracted somewhat from his work performance and is "definitely not a plus [to work]," but he does not dwell on the impact family has on his career. He loves his kids, but his personal life is oriented around the prestigious calling of science. Of his work he said: "I do what I want when I want."

Another tenured professor of biology told us that, as he sees it,

> doing science [is] a privilege. It's not something that everyone gets to do. I mean, how many jobs are there where you get up in the morning and go, "What should I think about today?" and then get paid for that work? . . . I think it's an incredible privilege . . . and to be guiding your own decisions and your own plans. And so the trade-off for that privilege is that you pay for it in sacrifice, you pay for it in your energy and your enthusiasm because there are enough really smart people around that are willing to devote themselves to this. . . . This is too competitive a field to be able to be productive working at it part-time.[18]

Yet these were rare cases. Instead, we found that the majority of scientists today no longer match up to the image of the ideal scientist who is totally and completely devoted to research.

Academic science is deeply connected to family life at the level of institutional logics and structural realities. Although family life and changes to family life (such as women's increasing share within the workforce and greater contributions to family income,[19] the rise in female primary breadwinning,[20] and men's increasing commitment to the nurturing aspects of child care) have an influence on all professional careers, family life and the scientific life have a unique relationship. The length of training for academic science is considerably longer than the training period for professional careers with comparable prestige, such as law or medicine, and the ticking of the tenure clock matches the biological clock. By the time they receive tenure, most female scientists are near the end of their childbearing years and most male scientists are far older than the age at which the average man has his first child. Among all academic disciplines and all professions, scientific disciplines increasingly require longer training and more travel, core structural factors that impinge on family life. Furthermore, researchers find that, when compared with middle- and working-class occupations, the professions (such as medicine, law, and banking) have been slower to accommodate workers with families—and universities are particularly poor at accommodating family life; they are often far behind the corporate world in providing family-friendly workplaces.[21] Today, academic scientists must keep multiple complex tasks going simultaneously, which might in any one day include lab management, teaching, and applying for funding; at the same time, universities are providing fewer and fewer administrative supports. Additionally, increasing specialization and greater competition for limited funding lead to greater feelings of isolation and stress among scientists.

With the National Science Foundation (NSF) and other leading grant agencies funding a mere 10 percent of received applications and the National Institutes of Health funding only 15 percent of the applications received in 2011,[22] few scientists are immune to the pressure to find funding for their labs and research and the difficulties that come along with trying to secure it. Academic science demands total devotion from the ideal scientist, competing with the kind of devotion that families demand. Many scientists feel that valuing family means they are failing to live up to this ideal.

We explore the perceptions of career, feelings toward life outside work, and the intersection of work and family for scientists in two different scientific disciplines, physics and biology. We examine the disciplines of biology and physics in particular because they are two of the core scientific disciplines, yet they have very different levels of female involvement. The proportion of women is much higher in biology than in physics, where women's representation has remained quite low. The discipline of biology now has nearly as many women as men, although this trend is not yet seen in the highest ranks. In fact, about 50 percent of the assistant professors in the life sciences in 2010 were women, but among tenured faculty this number was just 34 percent. The contrast within physics is more extreme, where women made up 22 percent of early career assistant professors but only 8 percent of the most senior rank (full professors) in 2010.[23] Figure 2.1 exemplifies the difference.

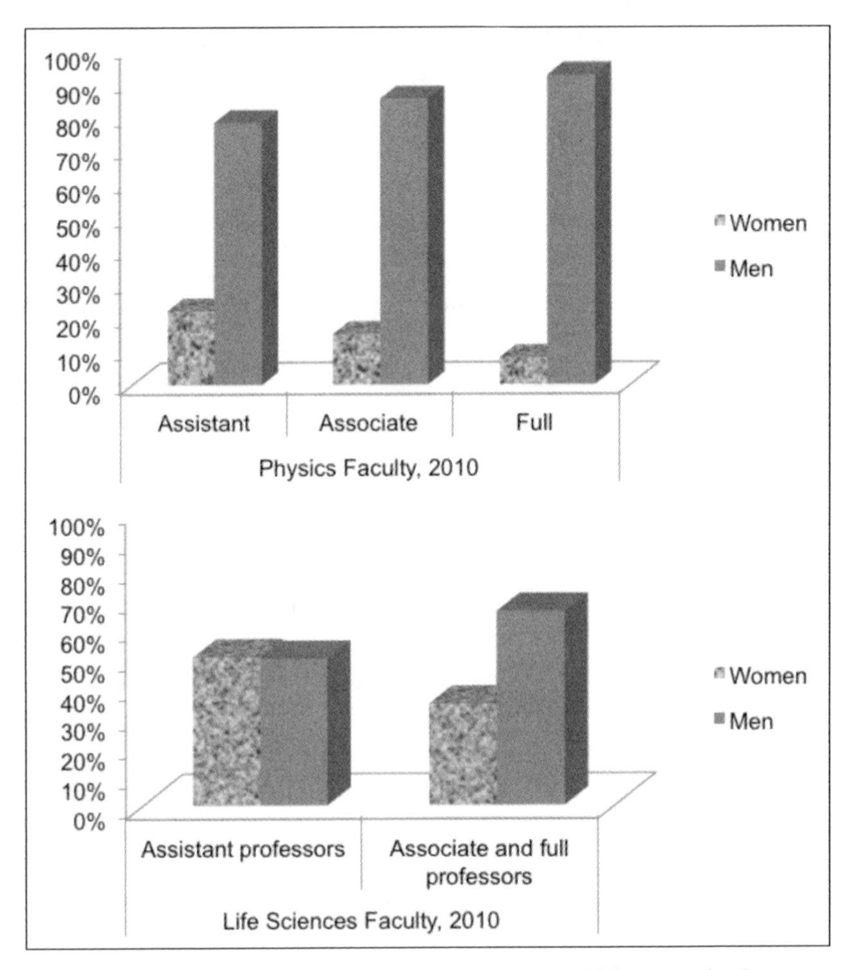

Figure 2.1. Percentage of women and men among physics and life science faculty, 2010.

Research on how experiences by gender differ between these disciplines is crucial as we try to understand how women experience the work-family balance, how family desires influence women's perceptions of their careers, and how perceived social support in the workplace influences women's career and family decisions. We must also look at the extent to which men in science struggle with the ability to balance work and family and how perceptions of stressors may differ between men and women in scientific disciplines where there are different proportions of women.

Researchers have recently focused on the forces that shape decisions to persist in science as well as on gender differences in those decisions. Family is an important piece of the puzzle. Since 1996, the proportion of those pursuing graduate degrees in science has grown nearly 63 percent for international students but only 17 percent for U.S. citizens, and most of that growth was driven by an increase in the number of women pursuing science degrees.[24] Among U.S.-born men, the attraction to and retention in science careers has slowed. By our calculations, using 2010 NSF data, women's enrollment in science and engineering graduate programs grew 32 percent between 1996 and 2008, the year we began our study, but U.S.-born men's enrollment grew only 5 percent during that same period. We find that family life concerns are part of why many young men either drop out of science altogether or leave academic science to pursue more lucrative industry positions.

Although women have increased their representation in science, there are still many more men than women in academic science posts, and it appears that academic science does not retain women at the same rate as men.[25] Indeed, although women and men currently earn nearly equal proportions of bachelor's degrees in science, scholars note the existence of a persistence gap, with many fewer women than men continuing in science past the bachelor's degree.[26] Scholars argue that concerns about family life are part of the reason fewer women than men continue in science. For example, one study of graduate students from 2004 found that women perceive more barriers to parenthood than do men and that this perception influences plans to pursue a future career in academia.[27] Is this still true?

Gender, Work, and Family

In some ways, the link between family life and academic science is typical of the broader link between gender, family life, and paid labor. Research finds that the gender composition of occupations continues to influence the experiences of work life. One study found that women in male-dominated occupations continue to perceive lower levels of support than do women in gender-integrated occupations.[28] The same study found that men in female-dominated occupations perceive relatively high levels of support. The conclusion from that study is not only that individuals are influenced by others' perceptions of what constitutes an appropriate worker for a given job but that those perceptions influence feelings of support in the workplace. In the case of scientists, then, women should perceive less support at work, since science has traditionally been a male-typed occupation. The cultural expectation that men put work first may explain the finding that both men and women in male-dominated occupations make more trade-offs that favor their jobs over their families than do those in more gender-integrated occupations.[29] Ultimately, research suggests that perceptions of support at work are tied directly to job satisfaction.[30] And researchers find that job satisfaction is related to satisfaction with life outside of work.[31]

Moreover, when compared with men, women generally report higher levels of intrusion by the nonwork sphere into their work life.[32] Yet the conflict between paid work and family responsibilities leads to lower productivity in paid labor and a decrease in family functioning for both men and women,[33] and is ultimately connected to feelings of imbalance between both spheres.[34]

Trying to balance work and family may influence the perceptions women have of their careers in distinct ways. Some scholars find that women and men place equal value on jobs in terms of income, occupational prestige, autonomy, job security, and promotion opportunities.[35] Other scholars, however, find that women's desire to have children and families is a key part of their personal cost-benefit analyses when planning where and how to enter the labor market. For example, women are more likely than men to plan employment around fertility decisions.[36]

Understanding the ways in which family life influences academic science and academic science influences family life is part of understanding the gendered nature of science. The assumption is that men and women drop out of science for different reasons: men for the higher incomes and advancement opportunities available in managing research or technical jobs, women because of family responsibilities.[37] Yet, in actuality, we know little about the stressors for academic scientists when it comes to balancing work and family, how they might differ by gender, and how they might ultimately affect decisions about whether or not to persist in academic science. Is the long-held assumption that family factors influence women in academic science more than men actually true?

There has been very little research on how the relationship between family life and science affects male and female scientists. The small body of research that does examine the relationship between family and work among scientists has focused mainly on the experiences of women.[38] This makes sense because women often shoulder the majority of family responsibilities. Yet it means we know even less about the extent to which male scientists struggle to balance work and family. Though family responsibilities may largely remain the province of women, scholars are beginning to find that family concerns weigh on male scientists as well, since they are often the primary breadwinners for their families.[39] Young male scientists also seem to see an academic science career as a particular risk to family time. Even those who are not yet in a partnership, not yet planning to have children, and far from caring for elderly parents worry about the impact an academic career will have on their projected family future.

Family Life Responsible for Disciplinary Differences?

Women make up a higher percentage of biologists than physicists; at the elite universities in this study, women constitute 43 percent of the faculty in biology but less than 20 percent of the faculty in physics. These are similar to the national figures we reported above. Any understanding of the relationship between academic science and family life begins with understanding the disciplinary culture a scientist works in. As one female postdoctoral fellow in biology observed, "Each discipline has a microculture that in some ways defines its membership."[40] These microcultures mean that even at the same university, biologists and physicists can experience substantially different work environments.

What do we mean when we speak of a discipline's culture? The term "culture" is used frequently, but without a shared, agreed-upon meaning. Culture can be thought of as a group's orientation toward common goals, norms, values, and beliefs; the meanings people assign to rituals; and the way people define social situations and themselves in relationship to each other. We found that physics departments in different universities had similar cultures, as did biology departments across universities, regardless of each institution's policies and practices. We find that biologists and physicists report distinctly different experiences when it comes to work-family dynamics.[41]

Some scientists suggest that it is simply more difficult for women to balance work and family in physics than in biology. One female graduate student in physics explained:

> The mentality seems to be different in the two fields. Not enough people have families in physics, and those that do seem to have partners who can take on most of the child care responsibilities. The sheer number of hours you spend in the lab count as a sign of dedication in physics. If I'm not in the lab, I clearly don't care (even if I am actually working). In biology, it seems that people have gotten over this mentality a bit.[42]

One female postdoctoral fellow in physics echoed, "Women are smarter: they know they are much more likely to get a job and build a family if they start a career in biology rather than in physics."[43] Another agreed: "Girls have the feeling that they'll have to give up having a family if they want to pursue a career in physics."[44]

Several respondents argued that physics is an especially labor-intensive and demanding field when compared with biology. They suggested that women might be particularly likely to leave physics because of family demands. They reasoned that women may think that physics departments, in particular, desire scientists who are willing to sacrifice family responsibilities, and as a result, women may choose to pursue a career in a discipline perceived as more flexible for family choices. A female biology professor suggested that in physics "women feel like it's too hard to . . . wear all of these hats. And so they've opted out."[45] A female associate professor of physics said the problem is "not going to be solved until we figure out how to help mothers figure out how to do the career and the kid thing."[46] Only one person, a female postdoctoral fellow in biology, argued that her own discipline is more time-consuming, saying, "Biology, more than physics, requires dedicated, long hard work hours and perseverance."[47]

When we asked one assistant professor of physics how being a physicist might influence her family-life choices, she told us:

> I mean frankly, I can't see how I could possibly have children. That doesn't mean I would have them otherwise. And it doesn't mean I couldn't do it. But I can't figure it out, and it is hard to say. I have never been somebody who was like, "Oh, I am desperate to have children." I can't say for sure that I won't do it, but I don't have any plans to now. . . . I haven't seen anyone do it in a way that makes sense to me, like anyone who has the career that I have. I just haven't seen it [*laughs*]. I mean, there are senior women who have children. There are not very many of them [in my discipline] obviously, and most of them then do nothing else. They do their work. I mean, if they have children and they continue their careers, that is it. And that is not the life I want now.[48]

We found that among biology faculty, 86 percent of men and 72 percent of women are married. About 18 percent of male biologists have been divorced, while 24 percent of female biologists have been divorced. Among physics faculty, 79 percent of men and 73 percent of women are married, and only 15 percent of men and 16 percent of women have ever divorced. Two-thirds (66 percent) of female biologists have children, compared with 58 percent of female physicists, while 79 percent of male biologists have children, compared with 70 percent of male physicists.

Is it really more difficult to balance family life with a physics career than a biology career? We found that the biologists in our study actually work more hours each week than physicists (fifty-seven vs. fifty-three). Biologists are also more likely to report that they think about work even when doing other things. Biologists, and female biologists in particular, are more likely than their physics colleagues to work on weekends and during vacations. Our survey data also demonstrate that female scientists in both disciplines work approximately the same number of hours per week; male scientists reported working just under fifty-five hours per week, while female scientists said they work just over fifty-six hours per week, and these results hold among scientists with children. Moreover, biologists are more likely than physicists to report lacking a feeling of support from their departments (18 percent vs. 12 percent) and from their universities (15 percent vs. 8 percent) and more likely to report that their careers have suffered from trying to balance work and family responsibilities.[49] There is some evidence that career-family difficulties may not actually be greater in physics, but the expectations in physics clearly result in physicists feeling greater tension between career and family responsibilities.

Academic Science Constrains Family Choices

A thirty-year-old postdoctoral fellow in physics, who is currently single, is extremely cynical about the graduate school experience and mentioned that he cannot figure out how he would begin to think about managing family responsibilities in the midst of the highly competitive academic science career.[50] Such a career is not just a day job, he explains, and it "will completely limit your family choices." He matter-of-factly explained that because science consumes all of a physicist's waking hours, other physicists in the same lab become the only readily available social companions. The eventual result, he said, is a situation in which "not only will you be cloning yourself in terms of your graduate students, you'll be cloning yourself with [the] life partner you end up with."

One young biology postdoctoral fellow, who is not in a partnership or married, talked about marriage and family constantly during our interview.[51] She said her upcoming thirty-fifth birthday "is killing me [*nervous laughter*] because there are no kids, there is no fiancé, there is no husband." She wants to have children but fears her chances of getting married are dwindling rapidly. She thinks she may not do well in relationships because in graduate school she has developed such a thick exterior that she finds it hard to let her guard down and be "feminine." When men have commented on this in past relationships, she has responded, "Science did this to me." She attributes her most recent breakup to the demands of graduate school saying that "things fell apart [because] people don't understand what you are going through in grad school and I think that goes sharp on relationships." With these personal concerns weighing her down, she feels that she hasn't recently been as productive as she should be and it has been increasingly difficult for her to maintain her commitment to academic science. She said that her family does not understand—but we do: science seems to have an enormous impact on family choices made over the life course, more so than other comparable careers.

A young biology postdoctoral fellow who is engaged to another biologist wonders if she will be able to stay in science because of the pressure the academic science career puts on life choices.[52] In her words: "The biggest detraction to having a career in academia is that very late during life—I think the statistic now is people are getting their first [major research grant] in their late thirties and early forties—[you are just getting settled]." (In fact, the age at which biological scientists receive their first major research grant from the National Institutes of Health has risen steadily from an average of thirty-four years in 1970 to forty-two years in 2006.)[53]

And then there's Jennifer, who was originally inspired to study physics after reading *Cosmos*, the popular astronomy book by the late Carl Sagan that was the basis of a Public Broadcasting Service TV series.[54] She is engaged to another physics graduate student who lives in a different state, and they spend a significant amount of time on the phone together every day, which takes away from their research time, she says. She told us about the difficulties she knows female scientists face when it comes to maintaining a family or having children: "Men can start families right away in their postdoc years, whereas women really don't have that option because it's such a high-pressure time in terms of being productive." There is also a trend toward achieving tenure at an older age, which means that it is harder for scientists to wait until they are really settled into their careers to have children. In essence, the tenure clock and the biological clock are in a race against one another.

To make time for family, some scientists change their approach to their work and careers. One male professor of biology, who is married to another academic and has two children under age five, said it has become too stressful to work on the weekends, and it's difficult to work after the children have gone to bed.[55] He has started to work less, trying to be more efficient, and noted:

> I think a lot of the things that we do are self-motivated, and so you're sort of providing an impetus for that, but at the same time, then you have to say, OK, I can't do any more work on this, on this project today, and so, in that sense, you sort of have to treat it more like just like a job—like, you know, if you're working at, you know, doing sales for some company, and you don't really care about the company and just that's your job. And that's, I think, an easier way of looking at it.

An assistant professor of biology in his late thirties said that he cut his workweek from seventy or eighty hours to fifty hours so that he could spend more time with his young daughter.[56] He told us: "From my perspective there, there is a psychological issue, right [*laughs*]. . . . I went from being, basically defining myself by my science and working really, really hard at it to where now it is a balancing act. And I think we are balancing well, but there is a cost to me [*laughs*]."

Science Challenges the Boundaries of Family

As we will see through the stories in the following chapters, academic science consistently challenges the boundaries of family life, pushing into the time a scientist might devote to children, parents, and other relationships. Pushing back, as we will see, often means a loss of work productivity.

An associate professor of biology, whose wife stays home full-time with their children, explained it eloquently:

> Most of the people in my neighborhood are not doing any work on the weekends as far as I can tell because I go out to the ball game and I'm the only guy there with a laptop [*laughs*]. So I think it's a quite demanding career choice and it definitely affects your ability to have quality time with your family. And for me, I think you have [to] make time with the family a priority and then decide how you're going to fit that into a busy work schedule. . . . When I was in my postdoctoral training and even in my first few years training in a lab, I used to be working six and [a] half days a week. And I think I realized when my eldest daughter hit age ten that was probably a really bad plan, that it was destructive to my marriage and bad for my relationships with my kids, and that it was not actually par-

> ticularly helpful to my work because it didn't make me that much more productive. And so for the last, I don't know, eight years, I have made it a point to be home almost every weekend. And so I'm here Monday through Friday and I'm at home all weekend, every weekend, with some few exceptions. . . . Now, the trade-off with that is that sometimes I work on the weekends. . . . And I also get into work early in the mornings, like today I got here at seven in the morning, and that's not atypical for me. And I leave at six thirty or seven in the evening, so that I'm here five days a week but I'm working eleven or twelve hours a day. *I don't know what other people tell you but . . . I think that is just part of the job—that it's not a forty-hour-a-week job, it's a sixty- or seventy-hour-a-week job for most people. . . . So I think it is a really, it's a very tough career for family and I think . . . that not only do scientists but also their families give up a lot to allow people to pursue this kind of career* [his emphasis].[57]

An assistant professor of biology expressed the same sentiment:

> What is hard is that a lot of really good science and good interactions . . . happen in conferences or over a dinner with visiting faculty, which we . . . especially at a top place like where I am, we frequently have some of the top researchers in our field coming through and we often have this opportunity to spend time with them, to have dinner with them, to initiate collaborations, to get advice. . . . [S]uccess is being invited to give seminars around the country or around the world, which involve travel, and you kind of have to do that in order to be successful. But every time you travel away or go to a dinner, that takes away time from your children.[58]

One physicist we spoke with believes the high demands of science contributed to his divorce from his first wife; as a postdoctoral fellow, he was working long hours—sometimes more than fourteen hours a day—as well as Saturdays and some Sundays, too.[59] He has since remarried and says things are different now. He spends more time with his kids, even if that means he doesn't get to read as many papers or write as many articles. As he shared:

> I think that's one of the biggest challenges in my life, that I had to sort of find a way to reconnect with my children. . . . [I]t's very easy to drift . . .

> [and] get absorbed by your work and you work longer and longer hours. . . . Of course, you learn, and now I think I have found a more balanced situation, also because my wife is also a professor . . . and she's not tenured, so I know exactly the kind of pressure that she's going [through] and I know that there's no other choice for me to do certain things and I have more time that I spend with my children. I take my daughter after school, we do more activities, but that is a big challenge. And that is something that I guess I regret—I guess I regret that I didn't realize earlier. . . . [A]fter the divorce, . . . I already understood that I was drifting from my kids further than I wanted . . . but again, as a scientist, it's also too difficult to understand how to fix it, right? So you go about it also as a problem: OK, here's the problem, what do I need to do? You read all the books about child psychology and, you know, you go to therapy, you find everything you need to do and then you just have to do it, you know. Coach this soccer league, go to math, volunteer. . . . I decided that this is sort of a more balanced life for me. So I have . . . commitment to my kids that is very, very concrete.

A famous woman physicist told us how family life has shaped her work approach and productivity:

> Oh, you become more efficient. And I guess it's true, you do. But more importantly, you . . . adjust your standard accordingly [*laughs*]. You just get more, like, "I'm not spending time." You just blow more things off. I guess it's part of becoming more efficient, but part of it is that there are things that I don't do to the same degree as I used to because I just don't have the [time], you know what I mean. There are just too many things to do![60]

And a famous biologist whose husband is a scientist at a nearby institution told us that she "worked *all* [her emphasis] the time" before she had children, and she would have been more productive if she didn't have kids.[61] "Now," she said, "if I had to pick between science and children, I'd pick the children!" Many of the scientists we talked to also said that if they had to choose, they would choose their families over their careers.

For a few scientists, the boundaries between work and family almost disappear altogether, and they actually find the two spheres to be generative to one another in some ways. As one biologist explained it, a scientist's work is

> so close to our heart . . . as are our children, that . . . it's just a little bit different than people who either have no jobs or have [a] job that they hate, which they're doing just for getting money, a salary. . . . As a scientist, I think we're always building. I have a wonderful lab, I have five people in my lab of graduate students who are just like children for me. I'm nurturing them, you know, and . . . I'm learning from them. . . . [I]f my grad student comes up with an interesting idea to do a test, test a hypothesis, it's just as exciting as when my son comes home and teaches me some new trick that he learned at school. For me, the pleasure is almost identical.[62]

Another physicist told us how having children has, in a sense, broadened the boundaries of his work, making him think more deeply about how work can change the lives of his children and have an impact on the wider world:

> When you have children, you're raising children, it makes you think about things a lot differently. . . . I hesitate to say that it makes you less selfish, but you're certainly putting someone else's interests ahead of yours when you have a family to take care of. . . . [A]nd so you start thinking about, well, maybe I should be doing research that's of more direct societal value, you know, or solve some real problems that our society faces, or at least do research that is more in that direction, you know. Maybe that's partly due to having children and sort of thinking about their future. . . . I'm sort of moving more into energy-related research problems at the moment, and partly that is because I see there are some really severe problems that need a solution or need probably a variety of solutions and it would be gratifying to contribute to that. . . . [H]aving a family sort of makes me maybe more sensitive to these sorts of problems that need solutions.[63]

Would stories like this, we wonder, be more common if academic science was more supportive of families? Can having a family actually help an individual be a better scientist?

3

Will I Make It?

Family Life for Young Scientists

Jackie is a physics graduate student in her late twenties.[1] She is energized and, in some ways, optimistic about a future in physics. She had an early interest in math and science and excelled in these areas. Her parents were supportive, and her elementary school math teachers were "encouraging," she says. This positive reinforcement pushed her to work hard in her math and science classes, and a high school astronomy course, taught by a man who had a doctorate in physics, solidified her interest in the discipline. The physics department at the large public university she attended was "very supportive of [teaching] women specifically," she says.[2]

But Jackie's graduate studies have been marked by frustration and instability. For one thing, she has "heard comments" and seen things that she thinks marginalize women in physics. When she began working in a lab as an undergraduate, her professor introduced her to male peers with, "She's the only girl in this lab—why don't you help her out?"; at the graduate level, the attitude has not gotten much better. At her current university, "there's a lab that's plastered with 'tasteful' pictures of naked women," Jackie said sarcastically. "If there was just one girl in that lab, those pictures would be down." While she "doesn't feel very welcome" in that entirely male lab, she insisted that she expected these kinds of experiences, and they have not deterred her from pursuing a career in physics.

What most discourages her, she said, is the bleak outlook for dual-scientist couples. Her husband recently completed a doctorate in astronomy in a different state. Although Jackie was accepted into some of the top astronomy graduate programs and was offered a multiyear fellowship at one university, she decided to pursue a doctorate in physics instead because she reasoned it would open up more opportunities for their dual careers, sidestepping the difficulty of finding two astronomy faculty positions at the same university. According to Jackie, negotiating two academic science careers has "staggered" their journey together. Now that her husband has finished graduate school and plans to begin a postdoctoral fellowship in a new city, they will live apart for "however long it takes" for Jackie to finish her doctorate. Then Jackie will move to be closer to her husband. As she described it, these complications have left them "postponing . . . where I thought we would be as a family."

Kyle, an easygoing biology graduate student in his midtwenties who gives off a surfer vibe in his T-shirt and flip-flops, is less worried than Jackie.[3] He said he originally considered going into sports medicine, but after taking an introductory course in biology during his first semester of college, he decided research might be a better fit. "I wanted to be able to do my own work," he said. "So it was kind of like a perfect career choice." As an undergraduate, he spent four months conducting research in another country, which gave him the opportunity to do hands-on work and see research all the way from data collection to publication. That was also where he met his current girlfriend.

When we spoke, Kyle was hoping to finish his doctorate in biology in the next few years and then search for a postdoctoral fellowship. He does not envision himself staying in academic science, however. He said that, in the long term, working "for a nonprofit, developing crops for Third World countries, would be ideal"—in part because of his desire to eventually raise a family. "I have a dog; he's kind of like a kid," Kyle joked, "but there is no way I want a kid anytime soon." The demands of his work and the difficulties of securing funding lead Kyle to conclude that starting a family "is just not convenient in grad school" and—given what Kyle has seen among more senior scientists—may never be convenient if he stays in academic science.

The experiences and perceptions of early career scientists are particularly revealing of the institutional, structural, and cultural issues that make it difficult for academic scientists to balance work and family. We discovered that many graduate students and postdoctoral fellows share the same issues, concerns, and feelings as they complete their science training at the nation's top programs in physics and biology. These young scientists often face hard choices.

The young scientists experience such difficulties mainly as matters of personal choice, such as figuring out how spouses can find academic science jobs in the same city so they can start a family. But apart from individual choices, the struggles to integrate family life with an academic science career also result from foundational problems in the structure of academic science in the modern university. Our research shines a light on these junior scientists, particularly postdoctoral fellows. Postdoctoral fellows often have a nebulous role; they are sometimes classified by universities as employees and other times as students. Sometimes they have no or few benefits, and they rarely have the kinds of benefits—like access to child care subsidies and extended parental leave—that enable them to balance family life with an academic science career. Yet, in the natural sciences at least, postdoctoral fellowships are now widely considered a mandatory step to tenure-track positions and have become the true "proving ground" for a future in academic science.[4]

After talking with young scientists, and comparing their stories with those we heard from more senior scientists (who have tenure-track or tenured positions at elite research universities), we see how both the structure and the culture of academic science needs to change.

Challenges for Young Scientists

Graduate students and postdoctoral fellows who are just starting their science careers face an academic environment that has changed significantly over the past fifty years. For one thing, it takes longer than it did before for an academic scientist to move into a stable career. Many scientists use funds obtained through competitive grants to operate their research agendas (and, in some cases, contribute to their salaries). Yet the age at which a scientist is able to support an independent research infrastructure has only risen. For example, as mentioned earlier, the age at which biological scientists receive their first major research grant from the National Institutes of Health has risen steadily from an average of thirty-four in 1970 to forty-two in 2006.[5] And the average age at which a scientist actually achieves a tenured job is also steadily rising, meaning that the stressful and demanding period before tenure is elongated, increasing the overlap with the time that scientists are likely to have young children. According to a recent report in *Nature*, "In 1973, 55 percent of U.S. doctorates in the biological sciences secured tenure-track positions within six years of completing their PhD's, and only 2 percent were in a postdoctoral fellowship or other untenured academic position. By 2006, only 15 percent were in tenured positions six years after graduating, with 18 percent untenured."[6]

Young scientists also face an academic environment controlled by an older generation of scientists who sometimes have different, often cynical, views on family life, having survived in the old system. As one young female graduate student in physics explains:

> The older generations are still in charge of the framework of the institutions, and how things like paternity leave (and things like that) work. I think that that's still a problem. I think that based on attitudes of men and women my own age, I think that it will probably change over the next fifteen years, as a lot of those people between the ages of sixty and seventy-five now start to retire. . . . [I]t's a very generational issue, even in terms of who will vocally discuss these issues in departments and who goes to things like meetings on how to change it or just research being presented on what the situation is. I think that people who are younger than forty-five are very active in those kinds of things, and people who are older are reticent to talk about it.[7]

Challenges of the Two-Body Problem

Many of the graduate students and postdoctoral fellows we interviewed made it clear that finding a faculty position in science is not necessarily their goal, even though they have devoted many years to training for such a post. For these scientists, a strong desire to be near family or have a family takes precedence over their academic career. One physics graduate student in her late twenties, who is dating another physicist, summed up the sentiments of many early-career scientists when she said that having children is one of her main priorities, and if handling both a family and a job in academic science proved too difficult, she would choose family over career.[8] It is not only women who worry about how the academic science career might impact their desire to have a family. *Many young men in science now share this concern.*

Among the young scientists we spoke with, both men and women talked about balancing work and family as one of the principal challenges of their careers. For a number of young scientists, this challenge

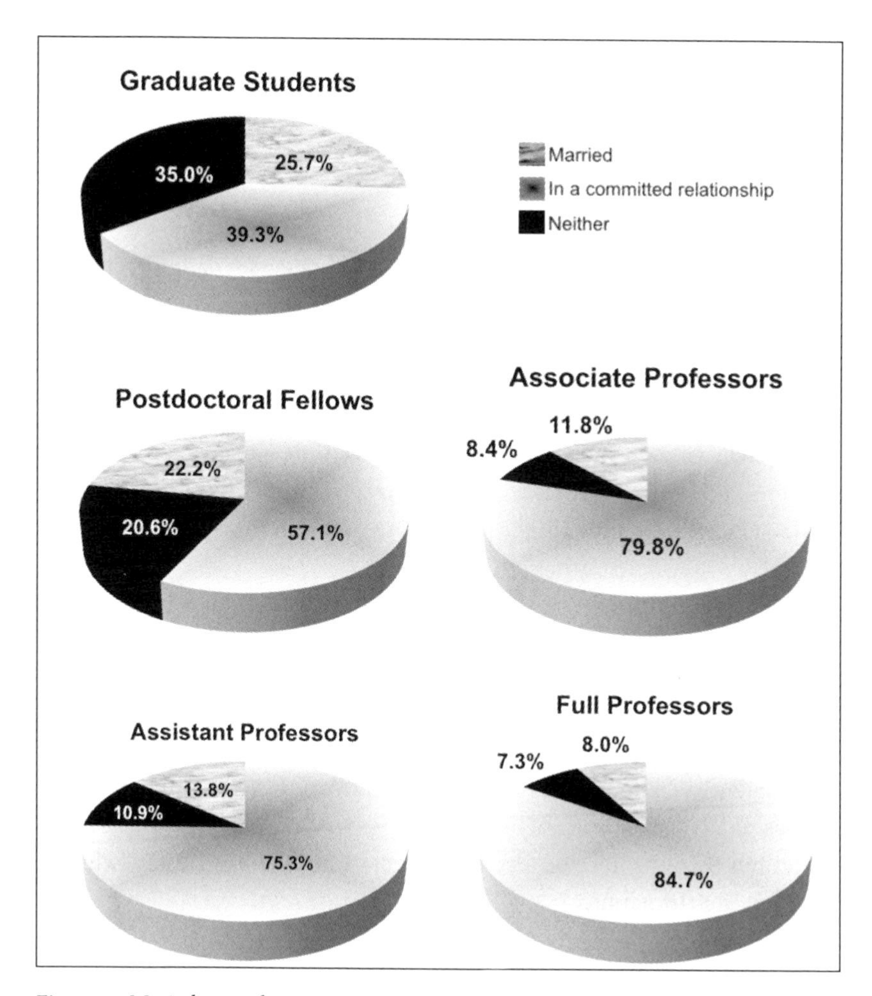

Figure 3.1 Marital status by career stage.

is exacerbated by the fact that they are married or committed to another scientist or academic. Of the graduate students and postdoctoral fellows we surveyed, Anne found that 70 percent are married or in a committed relationship (figure 3.1).[9] Within this group, 25 percent are married to a student, and 42 percent have a spouse who is also an academic. Nearly one in five (19 percent) are married to or in a committed relationship with someone who is in the sciences.

These scientists face the difficulty of finding an academic job in the same location as their partner. Although some researchers have found that having a spouse in the same field of science can—under certain conditions—be a benefit, the scientists we talked with discussed the situation in almost entirely negative terms. An astronomy graduate student in her late twenties explained:

> We call it the "two-body problem," being geeky astronomers and that sort of being a reference to orbital dynamics. . . . [I]f someone's dating another astronomer, it's really hard to get two jobs in the same place and one of them has to be really, really good—like a star that people will go out of their way to make accommodations for. And often, one of them ends up with not as great a job. . . . But there's something, at least to me, that I couldn't follow a spouse to somewhere they were already established. There's still too much of the feeling that everyone would always be thinking, "Oh, well, she only got the job because he was here."[10]

The two-body problem is often more complicated than two scientists trying to get jobs in a certain location—often involving intrarelationship competition and questions of worth. Certain fields, like astronomy and physics, are small, which means there might not be jobs for both this graduate student and her partner in any city. Moreover, like many other scientists, she worries that if she follows a partner who is already established at an institution, her peers will question whether she "got the job on her own merit." She also worries about how senior scientists will interpret her decisions.

The two-body problem is not particular to physics and astronomy. It also came up among the biologists we interviewed, and we found that it affects both women and men. While some researchers have argued that the two-body problem has much more of an impact on the careers of women than men (perhaps because research shows that women are more likely than men to leave academic science before achieving a tenure-track science faculty position),[11] other scholars have disputed this conclusion. For example, sociologists Kimberlee Shauman and Yu Xie argue that being in a two-scientist marriage does not harm the careers of women significantly more than it does men (although they do find there is a penalty to the science career for motherhood, a topic we will explore later).[12] Some research finds that women in dual-career academic marriages are actually more productive. In a 1987 study, Jonathan

R. Cole and Harriet Zuckerman found that female "scientists married to scientists publish, on average, 40 percent more than women who are married to men in other occupations."[13] Yet there is still a *perception* that when a male-female scientist couple works at the same university, *she* got there because of *him*.

Among the young male physicists and biologists we interviewed, many of those with a spouse or girlfriend in an academic career mentioned the ways in which their relationship affects how they think about their own career and, in particular, their possibilities for success in science. A physics graduate student in his midtwenties said that he has not yet married his fiancée, who is completing graduate studies in the humanities, because they are geographically separated.[14] As a result, he has accelerated his graduation so they will both be done at the same time and can look for jobs together. But he realizes that since they will both be looking for academic positions, and they want to be in the same location, her choices will limit his job choices; his fiancée's career aspirations influence how he thinks about his own future academic job prospects.

"My Research Is in a Race against My Fetus"

The time it takes to achieve a tenure-track faculty position strongly influences how young scientists think about starting a family. In many science disciplines, the training period—the time it takes to get a doctorate—is much longer than the training in nearly any other professional field. Doctoral work generally lasts six to eight years, and postdoctoral fellowships can take another four or five years, or even longer. While young scientists are still working toward securing a faculty position, their peers in other professions are often already established in their careers and have children in grade school. Scientists may be in their late thirties or early forties by the time they achieve the coveted tenure-track faculty position, if they achieve it at all.

Mary Ann Mason and her colleagues found that women across academia are having children earlier than their predecessors, yet mentors often advise young scientists against having children during the early stages of an academic science career. This means that many young scientists are in the arduous position of balancing graduate school or a postdoctoral fellowship with caring for a young child.[15] Our survey found that 7 percent of graduate students and 30 percent of postdoctoral fellows have children, as do a little more than half of assistant professors (who are at the beginning of the tenure track).

During these early years of training, young scientists have to be highly productive and publish work in academic journals, which makes it hard for them to devote time to other aspects of their lives, such as raising a family. A biology postdoctoral fellow in her early thirties, pregnant with her first child, says she feels a constant pressure to maintain a high level of productivity.[16] With a baby on the way, she has shifted into overdrive. As she described it:

> So I'm due in two months, and I feel like my research is in a race against my fetus at this point. I've set up so many experiments, and I'm working twelve-hour days every day, and I will be until I have to go on leave because I'm just trying to get everything done. So I do feel like I'm superproductive right now, but I have to be.

When asked how long she plans to stay in her current fellowship, she said the time span for postdoctoral fellowships in her area of biology is "pretty indefinite." Given the difficulty of landing a faculty position in her field right out of graduate school, "most people have to do a postdoc," she said, and some people do more than one. Although she originally wanted to pursue a faculty position, she now feels that "as a woman, it just seems very hard, especially tenure track . . . it's a lot of pressure and it just doesn't seem so worth it anymore to me." She is considering a job in industry, which she thinks is "a lot more conducive to having a family." In her view, the decision to have a child while a postdoc was a symbolic strike against her academic science career. "If I were a man, I wouldn't really have a problem with staying on a tenure track," she said. "My husband wants to do a tenure-track position if he can get one, and he has no qualms about that. He doesn't think he'll have to sacrifice anything to have more kids." As she explained, "I have to do the maternity leave and stuff like that, and he doesn't"; as she sees it, "You can't go on maternity leave and be on a tenure-track position."

Looking back, a young postdoctoral fellow in physics believes the postgraduate system is not set up very well for raising a family.[17] As she explained:

> You do a postdoc somewhere for a couple years and you do a postdoc somewhere else for a couple years, and you want to have a wide . . . variety of places to show that you have a diverse background and interact with people across the world. . . . [F]or me, [this] is going to be the time between when I'm twenty-eight and thirty-three that I'm hopping around doing postdocs . . . [so] it's not the kind of thing where you can say, "OK, yeah. I'm going to have a baby now."

To have a child, she said, she would have to "think about it consciously" and plan years in advance. Not only does she feel that having children poses a timing challenge, but in physics, she said, "regardless if you're male or female, it's assumed your spouse is going to be able to take care of [your kids]." Yet, she observed, "[it] always ends up being that the woman's career tends to be the one that gets sacrificed." Unwilling to take this risk and unable to maintain geographic stability, she is opting to forgo children and pursue her career.

It is not just women, however, who talk about how the rigor, length, and expectations of academic science training impact their ability to have a family when they want. Consider Kyle, who would like to have children but believes he has to wait until he is further along in his career. He also acknowledges that, given the structure of academic science, he may have to leave academic science altogether to start a family. In his words:

> If you're going the academic route, then you have to get tenure and you have that seven-year period after you finish your postdoc. So by the time you're done with that, you're forty years old already. . . . If you're planning on going into any other sort of nonprofit world, into industry, it's not going to be near as much of a problem.

Along with the timing problem, there are also financial concerns. During their training years, young scientists often do not make enough money to support children. Graduate students often have family incomes that are at or near the poverty line. The graduate students we surveyed earned less than $40,000 per year on average, while postdoctoral fellows generally earned between $40,000 and $50,000 per year (table 3.1).

TABLE 3.1. Academic Scientist (Physics and Biology) Salaries by Career Stage (%)

Career Stage	Below $40,000	$40,000–49,999	$50,000–59,999	$60,000–69,999	$70,000+
Graduate students	96.1	1.3	1.0	0.9	0.6
Postdoctoral fellows	20.4	43.1	24.9	8.2	3.0
Assistant professors	17.3	9.7	6.0	7.6	59.5
Associate professors	16.5	8.6	10.8	9.2	54.9
Full professors	0	0	0	2.9	97.1

One clear impediment to having children as a graduate student or postdoctoral fellow is the sheer cost—especially when we consider the expensive cities in which many of the top graduate programs in biology and physics are located (University of California, Berkeley, in the San Francisco Bay Area and Columbia University in New York City, for example). This factor is especially salient for graduate students and postdoctoral fellows who are married to someone who is also in the training years of an academic science career. And keep in mind that those we studied actually are in graduate programs or work at the top institutions in their fields, where stipends and salaries are probably higher than elsewhere.

For example, a married physics graduate student in his late twenties says he is waiting to have children because "supporting two people on the grad student salary is already pretty tight. . . . [In terms of money], kids probably aren't going to work before I am out of grad school, and so there is a restriction there. That's one of the biggest things."[18] When asked whether there is anything he can think of that would make his life better, he simply responds, "More money."

Lack of University Structural Supports for Young Scientists

Many top universities have an increasing number of support systems in place to help academic scientists manage families and high-level careers—such as paid maternity (or paternity) leave, adding more time to the tenure clock when children are born, and on-campus day care; of the thirty-one universities in our sample, twenty of them—roughly two-thirds—offer some sort of family leave beyond the twelve workweeks of unpaid leave required by the 1993 Family and Medical Leave Act. Yet many of these supports are either unavailable or not financially feasible for graduate students and postdoctoral fellows. As a result, those scientists who decide to have children while in their training years often find it incredibly difficult to maintain their careers at a high level. We also found that graduate students and postdoctoral fellows tend to feel it is not acceptable to discuss this lack of support.

Some young scientists told us that the dearth of such structural supports is what keeps them from having children at this career stage. According to one physics graduate student in her late twenties, the child care provided by her university is scant, with a waiting list that is "enormous."[19] A graduate student a couple of years ahead of her said she "copes" with child care by having "her mother and her sister coming over here for months at a time." She believes that if the university cannot provide adequate child care, it should at least help parents connect to low-cost, convenient off-campus child care. On the bright side, the child care situation at her university has pushed some graduate students to demand greater supports for families. For example, she said, "We're trying to get lactation rooms here because [my friend] stopped nursing her kid because she didn't feel like she could do it at the office." Another physics graduate student pointed out that, at her university, there is no formal policy regarding family leave for young scientists, which means they are at the mercy of whether or not an adviser is personally supportive of family life.[20] In her words: "A couple of the girls in my class have gotten pregnant and have kids, and it's worked out well for them, but it could have worked out very poorly because there's really no policy . . . there's nothing official." The underlying problem, she explained, is that "graduate students aren't really considered employees of the university, so . . . we fall into kind of a strange gap. We're not really considered students, but we're also not really considered employees, so there's a gap when it comes to things like that."

Cultural Shifts for Young Scientists

The difficulties that young scientists see their mentors and advisers facing in order to achieve success at the country's top research universities are making some of them wary about a career in academic science. Scientists at these universities must keep multiple complex tasks going at the same time, which in any one day might involve lab management, teaching, applying for funding, and outreach. To junior scholars, the work life of tenure-track and early tenured professors (those who are closer in age to these scholars-in-training) is often no more appealing than the work lives of senior faculty. There is increasing pressure to publish as many scientific articles as possible. There is also enormous pressure to procure grants to fund their labs and research—the only way to build an infrastructure that will meet the growing demand for publication. With only a small percentage of grant applications receiving funding, few scientists can escape the difficulties of finding funding and the stress that comes along with it.[21]

Today's graduate students and postdoctoral fellows at the country's top research universities are hardworking like their mentors, with an equal passion for science, yet they often have different personal goals than their predecessors did. Although they want to succeed in science, many express a reluctance to give up as much time with family as is expected in order to do so.

Young Men Want to Spend Time with Their Families

Young male scientists seem to want *more* than an academic science career, and an increasing number of them are in dual-career relationships, often with another academic scientist. As we found through conversations with many young male scientists, the cultural understanding of what it means to be a successful male scientist is shifting, and they want the institutional model of the ideal scientist to shift with it. In their view, they want the ideal scientist to be someone who is committed to academic science *and* his children. He seeks balance between his career and family life.

Over the past fifty years, men have increased the amount of time they spend at home—time-use diaries show that husbands have tripled the amount of time spent caring for their children since 1954[22]—and male professionals increasingly report work-family conflict.[23] "I don't think I would want to have my boss's job," one male biology graduate student told Elaine at the beginning of his interview without any prompting.[24] His boss, he said, is "constantly trying to secure funding and getting grants and writing papers . . . it's a lot of writing . . . and a lot of managing" that doesn't seem to leave time for much else. As this student elaborated:

> I mean, he's got to be in his early forties, I think. . . . He is young. He only got here a year before I got here, a year and a half. He just got tenure. But he's not married. . . . I don't get the feeling that he has a lot of personal time. I think that part of that is that push as a young investigator to get a lot of work done, to prove yourself so that you can get tenure.

Kyle, too, expressed unwillingness to become like his adviser, who is currently on the tenure track:

> I see the hours he has to put in for this, and I see the dedication that he really wants to be doing for it, and I do not want that to be my entire life, you know. I don't want science to be everything I do. . . . [I]f your number one objective in life is contributing to something in the future and making a big legacy for yourself—he is an amazingly smart man, he will contribute a lot to the future, and I am glad there are people out there like him. But those people aren't exactly like me.[25]

While Kyle acknowledges the benefits and job security that come with gaining tenure, he thinks the sacrifices required to get there might be too great for him. He doesn't want his entire life to revolve around his work, as it does for so many of his colleagues. He told us: "The moral of the story is: stay the heck away from really good prestigious schools if you want to have a life outside. If you look here . . . our entire ecology staff is people that are married to each other because they are here and basically their lives are here." Many young male scientists worry about how the demands of the tenure track might impact their current or future family lives, and they consider leaving academia as a result. One biology graduate student said that, among the scientists at the top research university where he is studying, "I look around and I see sort of two types of people."[26] He continued, "I see some people that manage, that seem to manage, to be really great parents and be able to sort of handle juggling everything, and then I see some people that sort of look stressed and over-into their work and sort of neglecting [their families]." He thinks it would be incredibly difficult for him to maintain an academic science career alongside an active family life, and thus he is considering a government job instead.

Many young male scientists reported working fewer hours than they believed necessary to be at the very top of their field, and they attributed these reduced hours to other commitments. "I'm probably not as productive as I could be if I was willing to make more sacrifices outside of work," a postdoctoral fellow in biology explained. "It's a conscious decision that me and my wife have made—that [since] I'm not single, I can't spend every waking hour up here, and I'm happy with that, with that decision."[27] Many of the male scientists who say they restrict their work hours view it as the cost that comes with investing time in their families and children—and they are comfortable paying this price. For them, spending less time with their children for the sake of their work would be too great a cost. As we see in figure 3.2, male graduate students and postdoctoral fellows who have children work significantly fewer hours than do their childless male peers.

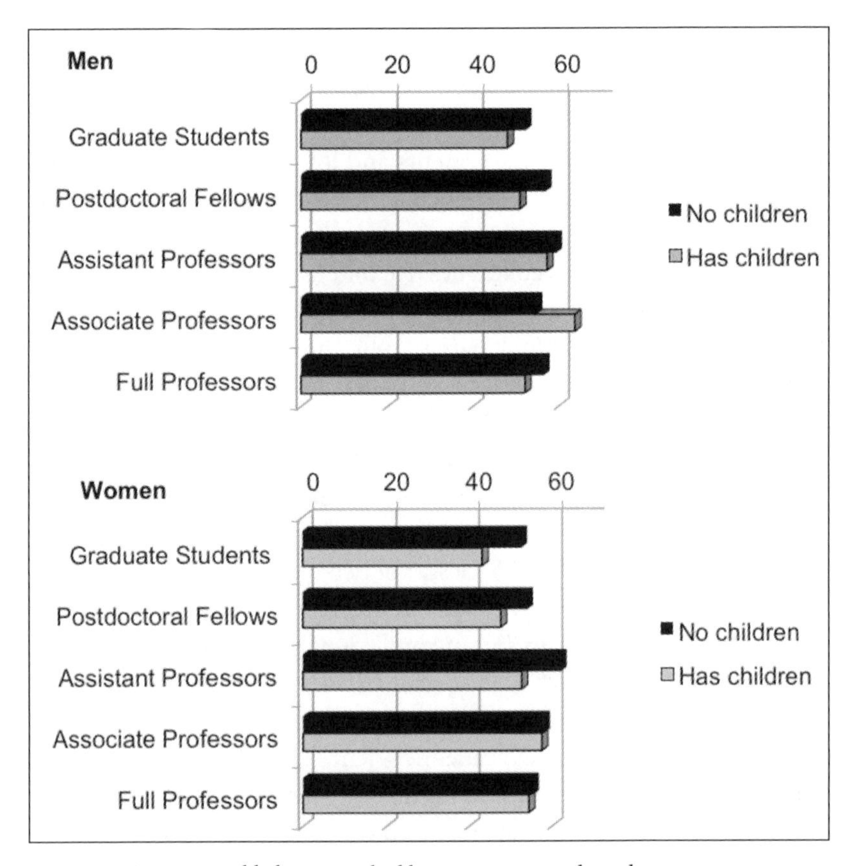

Figure 3.2. Average weekly hours worked by career stage and gender.

Young Women Are Not Willing to Do Science "At Any Cost"

The young female scientists we interviewed often said they see themselves as distinctively different from the previous generation of female academic scientists—the steely few who "made it" in science against all odds and often in the face of constant overt and covert discrimination. In response to an open-ended survey question that asked how men and women differ in their ability to balance work and family, a female graduate student in physics wrote:

> The senior women in my department do not have children, and half are unmarried. It seems that women still have to choose between family and high-powered scientific careers (at Research I schools) more than men do. The senior men in my department have wives who took care of house and kids and followed them around the country while the men pursued their careers.[28]

In the view of young female scientists today, the generation of women who came before them was willing (or had no choice but) to forgo relationships and children for the sake of an academic science career. Although these young female scientists respect and are thankful for the women who paved the way, they admit that they are not willing to make the same kind of sacrifices. They want to achieve success as academic scientists, but they want to couple these achievements with meaningful partnerships and family lives.

Young female scientists today hope to make it in academic science while holding on to family and other life pursuits. As one of the physics graduate students introduced earlier stated:

> I want to do this, but not at any cost. . . . [T]he older generation of women, I think, made it by doing it at any cost, but I'm not willing to do that, and so at every stage, it's sort of, "OK, is this a price I can live with?"—the sort of quality of life and being where I want to be and near the people I want to be near.[29]

When asked how an academic science career might impact her family life choices, a twenty-five-year-old biology graduate student explained:

> It's generally a negative impact because you see very successful scientists that do have families, but the impression I get is that they had to work very hard to make both work and that they needed—or were fortunate enough or savvy enough—to have a partner able to help them with their life choices and then with raising a family. . . . I am biased slightly because my [principal investigator], she's married but she doesn't have any children, and I know that personally she . . . doesn't think highly of people who have chosen to have children during an important part of their career. . . . But within my department, there are two or three young women faculty that have actually [or] are about to get tenure . . . and who have young children, and I see that they make it work.[30]

Here is the rub. This young scientist knows what she wants, and she sees it lived out among some of the young women in her department. Yet the perspective of her adviser—a person she greatly respects and admires—makes her doubt the feasibility of having children while achieving success as an academic scientist.

One young postdoctoral fellow in biology said she has sacrificed a number of extracurricular activities for her work.[31] She wonders if this is an omen of what she will need to sacrifice in the future—namely, her ability to have meaningful relationships and kids. She also said that she is about 90 percent as productive as she would like to be, but getting that extra 10 percent would require taking too much away from her personal life. Even her current level of work is not sustainable, she said. When asked to elaborate on this point, she explained that she has told herself that she will work this hard only for this time period. Although she is in her postdoctoral position to just focus on her research, she is not happy with her personal life because she is not in a relationship, and she does not have time to do much of anything outside of work. In her words:

> There is typically a small proportion of women that make it into the higher levels, into the professor positions, and they drop off along the way. But from what I've seen, with my friends, it's because they're in a relationship and they want to typically have children at the end of graduate school. They are in their late twenties or early thirties, and their choice is to either have a family or to continue on with their career, and they oftentimes choose family. . . . I put in probably sixty- to seventy-[hour]

> workweeks now, and I'm OK with that now, but I sort of wonder in ten years if I'm going to still have the stamina to put in this time . . . if I will have time to have children, for instance, and maintain a research program. That does worry me a bit.

A biology graduate student in her late twenties also said she doesn't do much outside of work, noting that, like others in her lab, she even comes in on weekends—not because she has to but because she wants to produce results.[32] When asked whether she thinks she would be married by now if she were not in an academic science career, she said yes, that friends in other jobs are married. In her view, going into industry is more appealing than a future in research, where so many hours of trial and error are required for professional success. A job in industry, she believes, would make having children more feasible, and it would be easier for her and her boyfriend to find work in the same city. As she put it: "From what I know, the famous women professors here, I think they don't have children—either they don't have children or they don't have a lot of time to be with children. I think it's like this, so it's up to you which kind of lifestyle you want, right?" As we see, in the culture of academic science established by their predecessors, young female scientists feel they have to choose: work in academic science or have a fulfilling life outside of work. It still seems nearly impossible to have both.

Why Stay?

Many young scientists, both women and men, say that the main reason they keep going on the long preparatory path toward a tenure-track job in the academic sciences is that they can see light at the end of the tunnel. They simply have hope that it will get better and believe they will have different structural resources and benefits as full-fledged scientists than they do as scientists-in-training.

Academia Provides a Kind of Flexibility for Having a Family

One physics graduate student in her late twenties said that she expects to have a flexible schedule as a university professor in the sciences, which might make it a good career for raising children.[33] "If I could do exactly what I'm doing [*laughs*] and split my time exactly the way I'm splitting my time for the rest of my life, I would be happy," she said. It is important to note, however, that the reason this young graduate student thinks she can have both a family and a high-level academic science career is because of a very particular local environment. Some research groups in physics are more accepting of family life than others, and this seems especially the case with her research group. As she described it:

> Sometimes [women who have children] bring [the children] into the office and no one cares, you know, and people are happy to see the children around, and so I think it's a fine environment for kids, but other experiments I think would not be as easy. . . . I think particle physics in general is easier than some of the other types of physics because [in other types of physics] a lot of them do a lot more hardware work and you have to be in the lab every day, but most of what I do can be done from home.

In her area of physics, she thinks she could "stay home most days of the week" and perhaps "come in to work a couple days of the week," and she wouldn't need to do a lot of traveling. A male scientist who works on her current experiment is married to one of the department chairs at the university, and while he is not a tenure-track or tenured faculty member, he has a lot of flexibility. As this student explained:

> He at first was a stay-at-home dad and then kind of started to go crazy staying at home, so my adviser had been alerted that: Oh, there's this guy here and he's really smart and he's in our field, but right now is a stay-at-home dad; you might want to, you know, offer him some sort of part-time flexible position. He has since come on full-time and he's really good actually. I think he is one of the smartest people on our experiment. But every day, he leaves at 2:45 p.m. because he has to get his kids from school. . . . [A]nd that's OK, everyone is OK with that, no one minds, no one complains; it's what he does.

This physics graduate student was one of the very few young scientists interviewed who discussed how the academic science career might provide a kind of flexibility that benefits family life. However, it is not the overall structure of academic science that gives her hope of raising children while maintaining her career, but rather the particulars of her local environment. Flexibility in a scientist's schedule is often highly contingent on the culture of the specific laboratory, research group, or area of science in which that scientist works.

In biology, a young postdoctoral fellow with a one-year-old son said she too believes that in an academic job you can be

> somewhat flexible, [in a way] that some other parents might not be able to—that you could say, "OK, well, I'll leave work at three and go to the soccer game and then will go back to work after dinner." So, you know, where somebody who has to be there in between nine and five, then they would miss the soccer game or whatever. You know, I feel like in some ways it's hard, it's harder, but in some ways, it's nice because . . . there are a lot of things about it that are flexible.[34]

Yet this postdoctoral fellow also highlighted the importance of the proximate environment, pointing out that her adviser is pretty understanding that she has a life outside of work. She realizes that the kind of flexibility she and the other members of her lab enjoy is dependent on how flexible their adviser makes the work that they do. Her boss makes the point "that people should be getting out and doing other things besides just working," she said, "so I like that. I like that this is part of my boss's attitude."

Other scientists also emphasized the difference a supportive adviser can make when it comes to how flexible their work schedule can be. A twenty-nine-year-old biologist in graduate school who recently gave birth said her university's maternity leave policy and efforts to help students deserve a lot of credit, and she has been able to reduce her work hours.[35] Her department and graduate program have been very supportive, she said, and key to this support is her adviser, who encourages her and her husband, a fellow academic, to pursue jobs in academia while having children. As this student said, referring to her adviser, "He himself with his wife are both scientists—they're great scientists. . . . So they tell me, like: You know, you can lead such a life; you will probably sacrifice things like cocktail parties, things like that, but you can be a scientist—both scientists—with a family." This biologist has found a mentor and role model that many of the other young female scientists we spoke with seem to lack. As we see, if an adviser personally values and encourages a work-family balance, it can positively affect how a young scientist feels about the ability to have both children and an academic career. If instead the adviser to a young scientist is an institutional gatekeeper who helps sustain a culture that severely restricts personal time, it becomes much more difficult to have a family while staying in academic science—and a much harder decision.

Why Leave?

Among graduate students and postdoctoral fellows in physics and biology, there is no gender difference in career satisfaction or number of children, yet a greater proportion of women worry that an academic science career will keep them from having a family (for graduate students, 29 percent of women vs. 7 percent of men;[36] for postdoctoral fellows, 12 percent of women vs. 7 percent of men).[37] Table 3.2 shows this more clearly.

TABLE 3.2. Percentage of Scientists Who Have and Want Children

Career Stage	Has Children (%)	Has Had Children, But Fewer Than Wished Due to Science Career (%)	Has Had Fewer Children Than Wished Due to Science Career (Includes Childless Persons) (%)
Graduate students	7.1	45.8	29.5
Postdoctoral fellows	30.4	36.5	45.4
Assistant professors	56.3	39.3	44.1
Associate professors	74.1	30.3	33.4
Full professors	81.4	17.7	20.5

It is not surprising, then, that by the time they reach the postdoctoral level, women are much less likely than men to report considering a tenure-track academic job at a research university (69 percent of women vs. 84 percent of men).[38] What is interesting, however, is that men *and* women who are training in science are roughly equally likely to report considering a career outside of science entirely (for graduate students, 26 percent of women and 25 percent of men;[39] for postdoctoral fellows, 20 percent of women and 16 percent of men).[40] Overall, nearly 26 percent of the graduate students and 18 percent of the postdoctoral fellows we surveyed reported considering a job outside of science.

We used statistical analyses to determine the factors that prompt graduate students and postdoctoral fellows to consider a career outside of science. For example, we adjusted for sex, age, race, marital status, number of children, weekly hours worked, satisfaction with life outside of work, and the fear that a science career would preclude having a family. Having fewer children than desired due to a science career is the only factor that predicts seeking a career outside of science, *and* it does so for both men and women: graduate students who have fewer children than desired are 21 percent more likely than other graduate students to report considering a career outside of science, and postdoctoral fellows with fewer children than they wanted are 29 percent more likely than their peers to report the same interest. There is no question, then, that this variable is worth the attention of university administrators who seek to attract and retain young scientists.

But might there be other reasons why young scientists are leaving academic science? As we discussed in chapter 1, economist Albert O. Hirschman explains that members of an institution will remain loyal to that institution when they disagree with its policies *if* the organization provides them with the opportunity to bring change.[41] As we have seen, most young scientists do not feel like they have much agency to bring changes to the academic structure. In-depth conversations with these scientists tell us more about how specific intractable problems make them consider leaving academic science.

Failure to Resolve the Two-Body Problem

In our survey, roughly 13 percent of faculty who are married or in a committed relationship have a partner who commutes to another city for work, and another 6 percent live apart from their partner entirely because they cannot find jobs in the same geographic area (table 3.3). Among graduate students and postdoctoral fellows, the numbers are much higher. Nineteen percent of the junior scientists we surveyed are in a commuting relationship, and an additional 24 percent live apart from their partner. The two-body problem remains a serious obstacle for young scientists.

TABLE 3.3. Percentage of Scientists in a Commuting Relationship*

	Graduate Students	Post-doctoral Fellows	Assistant Professors	Associate Professors	Full Professors
Living entirely apart in separate communities	26.1	21.1	9.0	4.3	5.0
One or both partners commutes regularly	16.6	22.1	15.1	16.8	9.2
Total Surveyed	**429**	**380**	**377**	**279**	**487**

**Includes those in committed relationships.*

As we have seen, more and more scientists find themselves in dual-career relationships in which they are married or committed to another scientist or academic. They may choose to go into industry rather than struggle to accommodate two academic careers.

One physics postdoctoral fellow in her late twenties told Elaine that, for her, there is nothing that compares to the excitement and satisfaction of discovering something that no one else has thought of. She has dreamed of becoming a professor.[42] But the two-body problem may lead her to take a position in a research division of a company like Yahoo! or Google. Her husband is currently a postdoctoral fellow in the same field at a university far enough from her university that in order for them to live together, she has to commute three hours each day—a huge drain on her energy and productivity. She knows of other couples with long commutes, but this is not what she wants from life. And in a few months, both she and her husband will be starting new postdoctoral fellowships in different countries.

They would like to have children, and she does not want to live in a separate city or country from her husband. She also does not want to leave academic science, but she anticipates that finding a research position in the same location as her husband may prove to be an insurmountable challenge. Thus finding a job in industry, she said, is "always something I toy with, but I've yet to find a really good position that would challenge me. . . . But I could find an industry job that I would find rewarding. . . . [P]retty much, I'm reserving leaving academia as a final choice to make my personal life work." She said that she would move to industry as a way of "ultimately solving . . . my two-body problem with my husband . . . if we couldn't find research positions together."

The Appeal of Industry

When asked about the differences between academic and industry work, the biology postdoctoral fellow who was pregnant with her first child answered that in academic science

> once you get tenure, it's great obviously, but women on those tracks, none of them have kids, or maybe have one, and have them late. So I do think that you have to sacrifice. . . . In industry . . . you have set hours, and you're not in a race to publish, so you don't have to work your butt off every single second.[43]

For her, it feels like a very distinct choice: "Do I want to do a tenure-track position or do I want to have a family?" She said that she will likely have fewer children if she goes the tenure-track route.

A young graduate student in physics reflected on the process of achieving tenure in this way:

> It's very, very competitive, which is one of the things that I think about when going into academia. I kind of take pause because, you know, the field is so competitive . . . in comparison to the private industry, [where] you would have a more standard workweek—but to be active in the research arena requires a significant amount of more effort . . . for less pay [*laughs*].[44]

Although this student enjoys the research he is now doing, he said that, at this point, "it's probably sixty-forty that I would go into research and development as opposed to academia." He is currently in a long-term relationship, and he believes a job in industry would provide greater flexibility for personal time. He cited his current academic adviser as an example of what he does *not* want to be. "He has two young kids and gets in [to work] at eight o'clock in the morning and leaves at seven o'clock at night," he said. "It just seems like if I had small kids like that, I would definitely not want to work that hard." He told me that although the freedom to pursue his own research interests in academia is appealing, "you end up working a lot as a professor and you want to have a family and kids, and it's a bit easier to work less and make more money [in industry] [*laughs*]." He seems to think that the greater flexibility and compensation he would enjoy in industry—which would provide him with the time and resources to raise a family—outweigh any "intellectual" benefits associated with an academic career.

He is not alone. Our survey found that more than 40 percent of graduate students and postdoctoral fellows at the top research universities are considering a career in industry, and more than half are considering a research scientist position off the tenure track. A smaller but still sizable group, 18 percent of postdoctoral fellows and one-quarter of graduate students, are considering a career outside of science entirely (table 3.4).

TABLE 3.4. Percentage of Early Career Scientists Considering Nonacademic Career Tracks*

Career Stage	Career in Industry	Research Scientist, Non-Tenure Track	Career Outside Science Entirely
Graduate students	42.6	54.8	25.8
Postdoctoral fellows	41.2	62.9	17.9

*Totals not reported because the number of persons responding to each question differs.

The problem is that academic science remains greedy—it wants all of a scientist's time, devotion, and commitment. For young scientists today, this is not ideal. They are concerned about how they might balance an academic science career with their desire for a personal life and family—a desire they are not willing to relinquish. As we have seen, if forced to choose, many of them—both male *and* female—say they would put family ahead of the academic career. *And we should not assume that being committed to having a family means a young scientist is a lesser scientist.* Thus, if academic science does not make structural changes to better accommodate family life for young scientists, and if more senior scientists don't support and contribute to cultural changes, there is a good chance that talented scientists like Jackie and Kyle will leave.

4

Managing the Controlled Crash

Arthur's physics lab is a busy place filled with worktables and equipment. Levers and other pieces of hardware are strewn about, and students move in and out, stopping by occasionally to ask Arthur a question or simply to say hello.[1] He seems to welcome these interactions. Arthur, who was introduced in chapter 1, loves physics and the students he works with. He was born in a war-torn Europe, and because he was displaced during World War II, he did not attend school until the fourth grade. The tumultuous experiences of his childhood, he said, taught him

> to be a survivor, and with survival, then comes confidence. I'm most likely the most confident person in this building—self-confident. I'm also convinced I'm the smartest in this building [*when he says this, Elaine laughs*] but that might not be true. . . . That's arrogant confidence. With that, you can do anything you want.

Arthur has been married for fifty years and has two sons, who were growing up while his scientific career was developing. Yet, the most difficult challenge to his career, he said, has been "raising the money to do the research I want to do."

When it comes to balancing work and family, Arthur explained, without hesitation, that his wife raised the children and took care of the household full-time—a contribution to his career success that he does not take for granted. When pressed to reflect further on whether he experienced any difficulties raising two children while maintaining a productive academic science career, he replied, "No, absolutely not. That's why you have a wife." As we listened to the interview again, it struck us that Arthur did not mean this to be sexist; he said it in a way that communicated genuine appreciation for how his wife managed and cared for their household so that he could pursue the high calling of science. He went on to say, "[If] you need to be a scientist, it's very helpful to have a very powerful woman. She was a CEO, a secretary. And you wouldn't believe it—she ran the company. The boss [meaning himself] only signed things. And she keeps doing this, still today!"

Arthur's story is very different from Carolyn's. Now a professor of biology, Carolyn was in graduate school when she had her first child.[2] "The *faculty* didn't even have kids!" she recalled. As a result, she said, "I just never wanted to apologize for anything. And so I never made excuses for anything . . . . I would run down the hallway to nurse my baby and then run back to be the teaching assistant for a class. I mean, no one knew I had a baby in the drawer in my [office]."

Carolyn is a storyteller who provided long answers to our questions, leaning forward and propping her chin on her hand as she spoke. She is warm and personable, and in her office, photographs of family and friends cover her desk. She is married to another scientist, who is also a professor at a major research university. He commutes four hours every day to and from his job, sacrificing his own convenience to help her maintain a successful career, balancing his work and family commitments. Carolyn believes her career would have been severely limited if her husband had not been willing to put limitations on his career. "The only way that I could have been able to do it is my husband, period," she said. "I could never have done it myself; I don't think I have it in me." She sid she "would never give up having a family, and if I had to choose [between career and children], it would be my children."

When it comes to balancing work and family, it is easy to see Carolyn as a success story. A midcareer scientist with tenure, she is a professor in one of the top biology departments in the country. She has a happy marriage and a husband who seems to be an equal partner in raising their children. Yet, despite her success, she has struggled to deal with the work-family tension in academic science. Making time to simultaneously pursue science and care for her family has been difficult and exhausting, leaving no room for work relationships, outside friendships, or increased visibility in her discipline. "I am basically always at work or I am with my family, and a lot of the time those are integrated," she said. There has also been a great deal of heartbreak, especially when her children were young. Carolyn vividly remembers the time one of her daughters asked why she went to day care after school rather than being picked up and brought home by her mother like the other children.

Some of the difficulties Carolyn faced are shared with all working parents, but others seem unique to academic science—such as the long, drawn-out process scientists need to go through to get tenure. When Carolyn was pursuing tenure, her goal was to "just barely get it," she said, by meeting the minimum expectations; she did not want to risk sacrificing crucial family time for unnecessary professional achievements. Yet, as she has advanced in her career and her daughters have grown older, juggling the responsibilities of being a parent and a scientist have not become any easier. Instead, maintaining the balance has become difficult in different ways. Her travel schedule forces her to be away from home far more often than she would like, and she seems to have even more pressures at work. Even with an established career, a supportive husband, and healthy children, balancing work and family is incredibly hard, and Carolyn is barely keeping her head above water.

Researchers and policy makers continue to be concerned about the gender gap in tenured academic science positions. Those who have attempted to explain this gap note that, for women, long work hours, difficult travel schedules, rapid proliferation of knowledge, and extreme competitiveness make a scientific career nearly incompatible with family life.[3] The argument goes that, because homemaking and child care are generally more the province of women than men, an incompatibility between scientific work and family life may be to blame for gender disparities in the academic sciences.[4]

So far, the small body of research that examines the relationship between family and work among scientists has focused mainly on the experiences of women.[5] What would we find if we deeply examined the lives of men in tenured academic science positions? Would the argument hold up? Are things truly easier for established male scientists with children? Are they all like Arthur?

James is an associate professor of physics in his early fifties who is married to another physicist.[6] Like Carolyn, he is highly accomplished, though he is at a slightly earlier point in his career. He completed his postdoctoral work at one institution while his then fiancée spent two years at another institution completing her postdoctoral fellowship. Concerned about the difficulty of finding two academic jobs in the same city, and unwilling to risk the stress and potentially negative effects on their marriage that could come from living apart, they chose to postpone getting married until they were assured they could live in the same location. Although they planned to apply for jobs together, James applied for the position he currently holds as a "practice" run and was surprised to get the job, but there was no position for his wife. So he accepted a visiting faculty position at another institution, hoping to use it as leverage to help his wife get a job. "The counteroffer worked," he said. His wife was ultimately offered a postdoctoral position at the school where they are now both tenured faculty members.

James is prone to acting on impulse and taking on challenges, qualities that are common among the male scientists we interviewed. When it came to starting a family while also pursing a career, he recalled saying to his wife: "'Oh, let's have kids, how hard can it be?' . . . You know, I forged much of my career the same way, 'How hard can it be?' And we all know that you just keep saying that until you find out how hard it is and then it's important to stop asking that question!"

Nevertheless, they waited until their careers stabilized before having children. James was forty when his first child was born, more than fifteen years older than the average American man at the time he has his first child.[7] When his second child was born, James was forty-three.

From the start, he recalls feeling that "it was going to be important . . . not to say [to his wife], 'Oh, and you're in charge of the kids and the house and we'll see if you get a job.'" Yet it has been difficult to balance a family with two academic careers, he said. Both of them joke that what they really need is "a wife"—a family member who could be committed full-time to raising the children and maintaining the home. But because they do not have such a family member, James and his wife strive to split child care equally. "There are many times where I have said, 'OK, you took the hit last week taking the kid to the doctor, I'll be at home today when the kids are out of school,'" he said. Still, he admitted that he and his wife might not actually put in the same amount of work. Uncommon among the scientists we interviewed, James quoted social science, explaining: "As social science studies have found . . . guys might think it's equal, but it's not." James does feel, however, that their relationship is "more equal than many others" he knows of, especially when it comes to time spent taking care of the children.

As a result, raising their two children has taken a toll on both of their careers. "The extra overhead of managing the home life means that we don't put as many hours in at work as our peers do," James said. Moreover, he has disavowed the geographic mobility often necessary to advance in an academic career, explaining that because he and his wife are lucky enough to have jobs at the same institution, "our next career move is retirement." Although they are happy about their decisions, James admitted that "neither one of us is as accomplished or widely published or cited or famous [as we could be] . . . because of our decision to have kids." It becomes clear that, even though he has had success, James believes his career prospects have been limited by his family life, just as Carolyn does.

When we look at research that examines tensions between work life and family life in professions outside of science, we see that men are less likely than women to deal with work-family conflicts by reducing work hours or making specialization trade-offs.[8] In fact, research that has looked at a range of professions suggests that men are actually likely to increase their work hours after the birth of a child, and men in dual-earner couples are less likely than their wives to restrict their work efforts after having children, although there may be exceptions.[9] For example, other researchers have found that men whose wives remain employed full-time may decrease their hours after having children.[10] What do we find among tenured and tenure-track scientists at elite universities today? How are they responding to work-family challenges?

Our research shows that both male and female midcareer scientists frame work-family challenges in terms of personal choices: Will I work fewer hours? Will I choose to spend more time with my children? Will I put family ahead of career? Yet we find that the range of individual choices available to these scientists is very much shaped by structural and cultural forces within academic science.

When Women Won't Give Up Work and Men Won't Give Up Family

Although there are certainly gender differences in the work-family challenges academic scientists' face, it is important to note that James and Arthur have vastly different family situations and work-family approaches, while James and Carolyn described very similar experiences. Together, our discussions with these scientists suggest that there are also generational differences in the work-family struggles of established academic scientists.

Today, most tenured male scientists under the age of fifty-five do not have a stay-at-home wife. In fact, science may be at the leading edge of professions with two-career couples. One scholar who studied the academic labor market at research universities points out that as far back as 1988, "the spouse employment issue is much more pronounced" than in other professional realms. For example, another survey from the early 1990s showed that 80 percent of faculty had a spouse or partner who was a working professional. Of the male and female scientists we interviewed, 25 percent are married to another scientist. In the new generation of midcareer scientists, both women and men must negotiate work and family.[11] Both female and male scientists struggle with structural barriers in the university setting that restrict their ability to raise children or care for aging parents while also participating in the kinds of activities their universities expect in order to maintain visibility in their area of science. This is why, even after they attain tenure-track faculty positions, academic scientists still experience acute tensions between their personal and professional lives. Even for those who have "made it," namely, those who have the most institutional resources available to them at the most elite universities, the struggles do not end. It is particularly telling that these successful scientists—those who have the most resources—continue to struggle with balancing family life and their academic science careers. Scientists at less elite universities (with fewer resources) might struggle even more. Moreover, these midcareer and senior scientists are communicating an experience of struggle to the early career scientists they mentor, which may lead talented young scientists to leave academic science.

Gayle, a tenured professor of physics in her midfifties who is in her second marriage and has raised two adolescent boys, described the tension between work and family as unbearable at times: "The balance is not possible. I used to say *I am in a controlled crash*, and I can say now I am in a semicontrolled crash all the time. You just have to roll with it. . . . I don't consider my job to be a job or a career. *It's my life*. I am a physicist. I am also a mom. And I am a wife."[12] Gayle places great value on all of these roles, and yet she wonders if she is "not the wife and the mother that I really should be, and not the physicist that I could be."

A "Male" Model That Doesn't Work for Women or Men

The culture of academic science makes it very difficult for scientists to place a high value on family life. The culture demands long work hours and an all-consuming dedication to the profession—generally taken as evidence of a moral commitment to science that is expected by a scientist's peers and superiors.[13] This culture stems from that fact that academic science was once the sole province of men, and elite men in all professions are generally understood to have a strong devotion to the world of paid work. This devotion dates back to the industrial development of the early twentieth century and even earlier, when the majority of Americans embraced a gendered dual-sphere model in which men worked for pay as the "breadwinner" while women worked without pay as the "homemaker."[14] Such a division of labor created a system in which men took on the role of "ideal worker," while their wives supported their employment—in both emotional and practical terms—by caring for the home or doing smaller, less significant jobs for pin money.[15] This model maintains deep cultural resonance in modern-day America. What emerged from the division of labor are certain cultural schemas—interpretive frames that guide how we look at the world and process information.[16] For men, these schemas "inspire, organize and justify career dedication," such that many men interpret devotion to work as holding greater moral significance than does devotion to home.[17] Thus, in certain work environments, such as academia, a masculine model of intensive work emerged—a model that now applies to both male and female workers.

Devotion to work is most evident among men whose careers demand long hours, travel, and the willingness to put aside other commitments (including those related to family) in order to focus on occupational tasks. Such demands are common among the successful biologists and physicists we spoke with. Devotion to work is also a form of normative control that favors institutions by incentivizing high levels of productivity and commitment.[18] This devotion is so accepted in American culture that it is even enshrined in labor laws. For example, the Fair Labor Standards Act of 1938 created a clear distinction between hourly and salaried workers, effectively allowing companies to avoid paying overtime rates to salaried employees who work beyond regular business hours. Companies consequently have incentives to encourage long hours among their salaried workers. Particularly relevant to academic science is the fact that long hours appear to be called for by academic organizations rather than sought by employees;[19] in other words, academic and scholarly organizations may demand hours that scientists do not necessarily want to give.

The following is what is really striking: the intense devotion to work commonly seen among men is also found among senior women scientists. This finding supports previous research that indicates that, in general, women are increasingly valuing their paid career opportunities. According to a recent Pew study:

> The past 15 years have also seen an increase in the share of middle-aged and older women who say being successful in a high-paying career or profession is "one of the most important things" or "very important" in their lives. Today about the same share of women (42 percent) and men (43 percent) ages 35 to 64 say this. In 1997, more middle-aged and older men than women felt this way (41 percent vs. 26 percent).[20]

In academic science, both men and women are expected to work until they find a "significant result," without regard for time limitations or other life spheres.[21] The constant pressure to churn out publications, accrue awards, and obtain grants makes scientists feel that their work life has no bounds, allowing it to easily bleed into family time. The irony is that there often appears to be an invisible wall that prohibits family life from bleeding into work time. The scientists we interviewed stressed that there is a definite limit on the extent to which family life may impose on their work life before questions arise from both superiors and peers concerning how serious they are about their scientific careers. For example, men told us that they are expected to return quickly to work after the birth of a child, and women said they are expected to appear as if having young children does not interfere with their ability to travel for work. In other words—even though it is practically impossible to do so—scientists must make it appear as if they are living the life of the ideal scientist, whose scientific work is the highest priority and completely separate from his or her personal life. In reality, however, scientists who are parents can never completely separate their two identities.

Even if scientists choose not to cover their office desks with pictures of their children, pregnancies become visible, children's teachers call at work, and sick children sometimes have no place to go except the lab.[22]

For Jill, a physicist who has children and knew from a young age she was interested in science, devoting time to intensive child rearing distinguishes her from her senior colleagues. As she explained:

> The very senior faculty don't have kids, and the way they have run things in the past is that they simply work huge numbers of hours to get things done . . . so when I came here, the flattering thing was the very senior faculty . . . were almost immediately talking about me being chair . . . within the next five years. Because they saw me as someone who would be a good leader but also a good organizer. [And] this was flattering on the one hand, but on the other hand it was very overwhelming because the way they have operated—I think because they don't have kids, so this is very stereotypical and selfish of me—they have just poured hours and hours into this job.[23]

Very senior faculty tend not to understand the sorts of struggles midcareer scientists face today because they ascended in an environment in which almost everyone valued and conformed to a male model of professional work (often because they did not have children or had someone at home to take care of all family matters). Therefore, when a woman like Carolyn has a child while in graduate school, or a man like James refuses to change universities because of his family, or someone like Jill turns down career opportunities because she wants to have time for her kids, their decisions appear unusual. Yet our research suggests that, even if universities do not recognize it, many midcareer academic scientists are making these kinds of choices. Today, ideal scientists like Arthur are the exception rather than the norm.

Personally Negotiating Structural Challenges

The Two-Body Problem for Midcareer, Dual-Career Couples

More than 50 percent of male biology and physics faculty at top research universities are married to a woman with a career at the same prestige level, and 21 percent of these men are married to a woman who is also an academic faculty member. Of the women faculty scientists surveyed, Anne found that 51 percent are married to a man who is also an academic faculty member (table 4.1).[24]

TABLE 4.1. Spouse/Partner Employment Status, by Gender and Career Stage from Survey (%)*

	Graduate Students	Post-doctoral Fellows	Assistant Professors	Associate Professors	Full Professors
Men					
Partner works	40.3	43.2	60.9	67.0	59.9
Has academic partner	36.9	30.3	30.1	34.0	28.1
Partner is in science†	12.6	10.7	14.8	14.5	14.4
Partner not employed or seeking employment	4.4	13.7	13.3	13.5	16.2
Women					
Partner works	48.0	53.8	86.4	89.2	82.3
Has academic partner	53.3	51.3	52.0	55.4	62.0
Partner is in science†	26.2	29.2	30.4	41.0	39.9
Partner not employed or seeking employment	0	0.6	3.2	1.2	1.9

*Includes those in committed relationships. Totals are not reported because the number of persons responding to each question differs.
† Includes private sector.

We find that the two-body problem persists beyond the junior career level. Given the structure of academic science (e.g., competitive job market, few jobs, universities often located in remote areas without other universities nearby), it is incredibly difficult for both partners to find jobs in the same place. For both scientists to succeed, they often have to look for jobs in different places—which often means dealing with long commutes or separate living arrangements—or one has to move to accommodate the other, which can, in turn, mean sacrificing career prospects.[25] But unlike in the past, it is not just women who are sacrificing their own ambitions for the career prospects of a spouse. Men are doing it too.[26]

Dual-career couples in academic science use a variety of strategies to negotiate the two-body problem. Some of these strategies are long-term, including placing one partner's career before the other's career, uprooting their family to accommodate one or both careers, turning down job offers in order to maintain a stable living environment, and temporarily living apart. Other strategies are short-term daily negotiations, such as taking on more child care responsibilities in a given week so that a spouse can finish a grant application or picking up a sick child at school while a spouse teaches a class. These strategies are not mutually exclusive, and couples who change universities for graduate school, postdoctoral fellowships, or faculty positions often utilize several different strategies independently or simultaneously.

For some scientists in dual-career academic partnerships, being in the same location as their spouse is the most important criterion for accepting a job. A professor of physics who is married to another scientist explains the process she went through when she was selecting her postdoctoral fellowship: "I had gotten married at that time and my husband was at that location, so it was the right place for me to be. A kind of simple, simple explanation."[27] Her words reveal that sometimes career choices are not made for professional or "intellectual" reasons (as might be expected in academic institutions that place so much importance on career prestige) but instead are made for personal, subjective reasons.

In some cases, what scientists see as a short-term strategy or temporary necessity can have long-term effects on their careers. Early decisions can lead to professional challenges down the line. As one tenured physicist in her late sixties warns, she came to her current university in the professionally insecure position of being a postdoctoral fellow in the department where her husband already had a faculty appointment.[28] As a result, her path was punctuated by several years of unguaranteed—what academics call "soft"—funding. Because of her nontraditional appointment, she later had to commute to another city to work at a separate institution, even though she had once turned down a faculty position far from home because, in her words, "we had little kids at home so I didn't know if I wanted to commute." This physicist says her tenuous, soft-money position "was fine, but it's not something that is a good, permanent solution, and unfortunately, as you probably well know, many women unfortunately get stuck in that type of position. And I didn't want to do that."

Other scientists in dual-career couples told us that even if they were able to take an extra year of school or a temporary appointment early in their career to accommodate a spouse, the highly competitive market for long-term, tenure-track positions is less flexible. To make it work, many middle-aged scientists conducted massive, national searches with their spouse to find faculty positions in the same location. To find two faculty positions in the same location or at the same institution, they very often had to sacrifice all other criteria, such as living near extended family. An associate professor of biology in her midforties, who is married to another tenured faculty member in her department, says she "probably went on fifteen or something job interviews."[29]

Finding two positions together sometimes requires a laborious negotiation process with a university that may be working hard to woo one spouse but is not necessarily offering a stable job to the other. A biologist in his midthirties told us that he and his wife are now both happily settled in tenure-track positions in the same department, but they did not arrive at their positions independently.[30] Obtaining two positions at the same university was largely the result of his wife's negotiations to find him a placement. As he explained:

> We were lucky enough that we actually were able to compare offers [and decide between two]. [We had] similar-type positions at another institution, and [this university] was definitely the better of the two offers, but it was definitely a challenge to make sure that [my wife] was getting all that she needed as part of her position. And in fact, a lot of her negotiating clout was being used up to find something for me. So that was a difficult situation.

Although the long-term implications of her decision remain unexplored, it is easy to imagine that she might have lost key research resources (e.g., lab space, sabbatical time, research funding, or salary) because she placed securing her husband a job at the top of her priority list.

Sometimes an academic scientist will try to find a faculty position in a city or a college town that presents good opportunities for a spouse who seeks a job in a particular field outside of academic science. That can also be limiting and difficult. A full professor of physics whose husband is an engineer said that her current city is a "good place for two-career couples," but "there aren't that many faculty jobs in my field each year—there are maybe five each year at most—so you know [*laughs*], you don't have a lot of choice."[31]

Several faculty members in later stages of their careers mentioned turning down—or choosing not to pursue—opportunities for professional advancement that would upset a spouse or children who were happy in their current location. Laurie is a full professor in her forties whose husband is a researcher at the same university.[32] They found jobs at the same university early on in their marriage and have been at this institution ever since. In part, they have managed their dual-career challenges by finding an excellent and consistent caretaker for their three children—a nanny who has now been with the family for nearly twenty years. For scientists like Laurie and her husband, the lure of searching for more prestigious positions elsewhere is hard to resist, yet such a change must always be weighed against family pressures and responsibilities. As she explained:

> My husband . . . was looking at chairmanship jobs ten, fifteen years ago, and I didn't want to move. It's hard to say whether that was because of my nanny, or if that was because everything was kind of going great for me and I didn't want to rock the boat. But I think that does play a big role, and I tell lots of women whom I talk to that [family] infrastructure is everything. Having everything very stable is what your kids care about most, and luckily I haven't had a bad work situation, so I haven't had to weigh the benefits of the two.

Often, the work of one spouse suffers when the other spouse needs to address a work-related emergency or major deadline, especially when children are involved. We found that both women and men make sacrifices for the sake of a spouse's career. For example, one assistant professor of biology whose wife has a demanding academic career at the same university explained that they "take turns, pretty much—like sometimes, if she has a grant due, then I will do more [in the home], otherwise she will. It can be tough at times."[33] Even after scientist couples have achieved tenure and settled in a location, balancing two careers still has its difficulties. The two-body problem may take different shapes and forms as academic science careers progress, but it never completely disappears.[34]

Whether to Have Children

In our survey of academic scientists, we found that 67 percent of junior faculty members who are men have children, compared with 57 percent of junior faculty members who are women. Among full professors, we found that 86 percent of men have children and 73 percent of women have children. It makes sense that full professors are more likely to have children because senior faculty members have had more time to begin a family. The gender gap evident at both stages is not surprising either, given what we know about how child-rearing responsibilities tend to be shared. It is also important to note that women scientists are more likely to have a spouse who works (71 percent vs. 56 percent of male scientists), and they are more than twice as likely as their male colleagues to have a spouse who is also a scientist. In our survey, we found that 13 percent of male academic science faculty members are married to another scientist, compared with 31 percent of women in the same types of positions.

When and whether to have children is a significant decision for any couple, but it has particular import for academic scientists. Although the tension between the biological clock and the tenure clock is most often discussed in connection with women's careers, the structure of academic science has an impact on decisions about children for both male and female scientists. Starting a family before securing a stable faculty job is often overwhelming, and in some cases detrimental. Even scientists with tenure-track jobs at elite research universities shared stories of needing to be resilient in the face of negative feedback from mentors about their family choices. For example, an assistant professor of biology, who is married with two small children, had her first child while in graduate school. She recalled:

> And then I started my postdoc and I had my second child [*laughs*]. So talk about stacking the cards against myself. . . . When I told [my postdoctoral adviser] that I would be leaving on maternity leave, his first instinct was, "There is just no way you are going to be able to do this" because I had two kids plus I had a long commute. . . . And in a way, I am glad he said that . . . it was like, "Who are you to tell me that I can't do this? . . . Well, that's not for you to decide." . . . I actually considered not going back because I thought that the road ahead would be difficult. [Academic science] is not a normal career, you know; it's not a nine to five, or eight to six even. It is like you constantly have to sort of be on, and this is a very competitive environment, since you constantly have to be in it.[35]

When asked how she seems to manage it all—two children as well as her work as an academic scientist—she described something akin to the "controlled car crash" feeling we heard about earlier: "I feel like everything is *organized chaos*. And sometimes I feel like it's complete disorganization because there is no real set schedule. Things come up. All of a sudden you might get these results or you have to do this [experiment]. [But] your child is sick so you have to go."

Tenured and tenure-track scientists said they sometimes waited to complete their graduate studies, finish a postdoctoral fellowship, or overcome the major hurdle of tenure before starting a family. One associate professor of biology, who is now approaching forty, said that before she went up for tenure, she "just felt like the demands on my time [were] so crazy that there was no way that I could think about trying to start a family and it wasn't even on my radar screen."[36] Another assistant professor of physics, who works at the same university where her husband recently received tenure and who plans to go up for tenure herself in a year or two, explained:

> I think that the problem is really about the time [it would take to raise children]. I love physics, but I am sure I would put more time in with the kids, and so I have a little bit of a worry about doing that before I get tenure because I feel like just to get tenure you have to sort of at least put the face on of being 110 percent . . . into it at all moments, and I think that will be hard for me.[37]

Her fears are not unfounded. At top universities, it is common for both men and women scientists without children to work fifty or sixty hours every week, with women working an average of fifty-nine hours per week and men working an average of fifty-eight.[38] These are more hours than many other professions require. Data from the nationally representative Current Population Survey show that lawyers averaged forty-five hours per week between 2006 and 2008, while physicians averaged about fifty-one hours. However, *both* male and female academic scientists with children report working an average of fifty-four hours per week, several hours less than their childless peers.[39] Over time, the extra hours that scientists without children are able to work may add up to more conference presentations and more publications, often leading to greater career success.

Yet as the path to tenure has lengthened, many academic scientists find themselves unable to wait until achieving tenure to have children, even though waiting would allow them to better accommodate family demands.[40] Evan, an associate professor of biology who is forty-nine and whose wife is also a scientist, said that they waited until he was "almost ready to come up for tenure" to have children because of the pressures of their careers.[41] Today, the kids are six and almost two, and even though the family has full-time child care and a part-time nanny who picks the children up from child care, he said it "sucks": "I mean, I am not nearly as productive as I used to be. . . . And it's hard because I used to do all the work here till whenever I wanted to and then I'd go home and I could work at night. Now I get home and put the kids to bed, right?"

This example is particularly striking because Evan *and* his wife are highly successful professionally. They both have tenured positions at elite universities near one another where their pay is well above average. Yet even in this situation—what most in academic science would see as the best-case scenario for a two-career academic couple—they still find life with children to be, in Evan's words, a "disaster."

Old Parents and Fewer Kids

Once scientists have achieved tenure, they often find that their busy schedules still make it difficult to have a child. One of the female biologists introduced earlier revealed that after she got tenure, she "sort of felt like, oh crap, you know, now I'm like thirty-eight, thirty-nine years old, and I have missed all this time when I could [have] been thinking about having a family, but instead I just knew at the time that I wouldn't be able to be a good parent."[42] She and her husband are now trying to start a family, even though she does not consider her current situation as notably more favorable for having a baby. "All of the crazy staying up until two in the morning writing grant proposals and writing lectures," she said. "It just never really seem[s] to let up." Once tenured faculty members do have kids, explained a forty-six-year-old tenured biologist who started a family after many years in a long-distance relationship, "the disadvantage of that is you're an old parent. You just don't have the energy."[43]

Though they are different in the details, the stories academic scientists tell about having children more or less contain the same overall message: having children in the midst of an academic science career is a struggle—no matter when you have them. There is no ideal time for the "non-ideal" scientist to have children.

Many scientists who have successfully raised a family while maintaining their career admit that they have fewer children than they would like, and believe that they would have had more children had they not chosen a career in academic science. According to our survey, about 45 percent of women and nearly 25 percent of men who are science faculty members say that as a result of having an academic science career, they have fewer children than they would have wanted.[44] Among the senior faculty in our survey, who at the average age of fifty-six are in the most advanced stages of their careers, 14 percent of men and one-third of women report having fewer children than they would have liked. Nearly one in five full professors have no children at all. Among assistant professors, who average not quite thirty-eight years of age, 35 percent of men and an astounding 60 percent of women have fewer children than they wished. Forty-four percent of assistant professors do not have children at all. Among associate professors, who typically have tenure and are in their midforties, 33 percent do not have as many children as they would want, and 26 percent have no children. We also find that female faculty members have fewer children than their male colleagues.[45]

When asked if she has fewer children than she might have wanted because of her career, an associate professor of biology in her midthirties who is divorced from the father of her eleven-year-old son replied, "Absolutely. I don't see how I could handle a second one. No way [*laughs lightly*]. This was enough. And there were moments when I thought, 'Oh I'd like another one,' but, no. I just can't see doing it."[46] She said that the first three years of her son's life were crazy, and she does not know how she got through them. At times, she would even write grants while breast-feeding.

A professor of physics who is married to a professor in the same department said that after they had two children, "We debated about having a third and then we just, you know, we just couldn't handle it. Two is our limit. I think if I'd had three I would've had to drop to half time or something. It's just—there is a point where you just can't do both."[47]

And an assistant professor of biology in his midthirties, who is married to another scientist and has children aged two and three, revealed how his wife's science career is influencing decisions regarding whether and when to grow their family:

> She's doing a combined MD/PhD, so the PhD is more flexible, but she's now starting medical school in the fall, and that is less flexible. So, we'd like to have more kids, but there are more, much more, defined constraints on when that can happen. And, I don't know how many more opportunities there are. I mean, it's difficult to be pregnant and to have a young kid when you're doing a residency.[48]

When couples have to live apart to advance their careers, it can also affect the number of children they have. One associate professor of physics who is married to a history professor said that they currently live in the same location, but for a long time "we were living apart—we had a long-term relationship for ten years, coast to coast—so yeah, of course it did, that delayed our family, and that's the reason we have only one kid to a large extent."[49]

Turning to our survey, we find that when we look at scientists with fewer children than desired and control for other factors, the women are actually *more* satisfied with their lives than the men are. This is surprising: it implies that having fewer children than desired has a more pronounced effect on life satisfaction for men in academic science then it does for their women colleagues; the men may experience more negative impact on how they perceive the quality of their lives than their female counterparts do. What explains this? It is possible that because women have had to break into work culture, they consequently expect struggle and sacrifice, whereas men have been socialized to expect "it all"—a work life and a family life that corresponds to their desires.

Practical Strategies for Balancing Work and Home

The majority of scientists today are not like Arthur—the ideal scientist who can easily balance work and family because he has a stay-at-home spouse who cares for all family concerns. Our survey found that about 31 percent of academic scientists are married to another faculty member, and another 23 percent have spouses who hold other managerial or professional positions. Only 15 percent of male faculty members have a spouse who is not working in paid employment, and less than 1 percent of female faculty members have a partner who is not working. None of the female scientists we interviewed have husbands who are at home full-time.

More Active Parent Partner

Elaine did speak with two women who are married to men who work from home part-time and who say their husbands are primarily responsible for child care.[50] One of these women is a tenured physicist with two young children, and her husband works flexible hours as an artist.[51] She has worked tirelessly at her career and says that she is "painfully aware" that "part of my success is not just me; it's who I married and my family." She adds, "I really feel that part of why I have been able to be successful is because I've got a spouse who is doing, at this point, more than 50 percent of the child care."

The other woman, Joanne, is an assistant professor of biology whose spouse works part-time in computer science.[52] At the time of our interview, she had recently given birth to their first child. She gets "a lot of help" from her husband and her parents, who live close by, and she is "sure if I had no help from my parents, and my husband was working full-time and wasn't very engaged in the child-rearing process, then it would be very difficult to manage a career here." Of the female scientists interviewed, these two women come closest to being the ideal scientist. They have family members who are able to assume a significant share of child care responsibilities, and within the current structure of academic science, this support plays a large part in allowing these women to succeed in their careers. But what do academic scientists do when they don't have family members who can help take care of the house and kids?

Delegating Personal Tasks Outside of Family

A professor of physics who is married to a professor in the same department shared that they sometimes must seek help from outside the family to meet their work and parenting demands:

> Both my husband and I travel a lot as part of our jobs. I have to [travel for research] and go to meetings, and you have to be on committees and be active [in your field of science]. So it was just a nightmare. Sometimes, one of us would be coming home from a flight when the other one has already left, and if there was a snafu in the planes—which sometimes happened—our kids are stuck at day care! We would be frantically calling someone to try to pick them up, but, you know . . . I had friends who really helped out. The parents of our kids' friends would often help out, and so it's really a network of friends that helped us through it, but it is a struggle.[53]

When such a network is lacking, balancing work and children becomes much more difficult. "We have essentially no support," said one assistant professor of biology who lives far from both his family and his wife's family, "which is probably the biggest challenge of all—the expensive care, I mean, putting [the children] through day care, the lack of family support because of being in a different city."[54]

Sometimes decisions regarding how to take care of children can cause friction in a relationship. In thinking ahead to when they might have children, one associate professor of physics wanted to use a nanny and day care, but his wife was against it.[55] She felt strongly that if they had kids, they would both have to be involved, and since neither of them was willing to decrease time at work, they decided not to have children at all.

Rhetorical Strategies for Balancing Work and Home

Academic scientists who have working spouses need many practical strategies to balance their career and family—making sure their partner is more available when they have a big work deadline, making friends with the parents of children's friends, and sacrificing work promotions to be with family. Practical negotiations are reinforced and propelled by the broad mind-sets that scientists adopt, the cognitive schema or rhetorical frames they use to explain their lives. The approaches to balancing work and family that they justify tell us something about what they think it means to be a successful scientist and a successful family member. In other words, academic scientists develop rhetorical strategies—ways of talking about their lives and framing their experiences—that explain the balance they have struck between their work and home lives.[56]

Family Comes First

Through their narratives, some scientists indicate that family is unequivocally more important than their career. They say they make their decisions regarding how to balance work and family within this framework and profess to "accept the consequences." Family-first ideas often prompt those with young children to leave work by a certain time each day so they are able to spend quality time with their kids. A number of both men and women in a variety of family situations adopt this strategy. Yet structural factors—such as whether or not the parent leaving the lab early is the principal investigator of the grant on which she is working—influence the ability to use a family-first rhetorical frame.

For example, an assistant professor of biology who is forty and married to a woman who stays home full-time with their six-year-old son said he makes sure to limit his work commitments in order to spend time with his family, even though he runs a busy lab and will submit his case for tenure in less than two years.[57] "I leave every day at 5:30 because I want to be home with my son and my wife, but mostly, my son is growing up and I don't want to miss that," he said, adding, "Of course, I get here at 7:00 a.m." He continued, "I don't regret [limiting work time], but it does slow down progress and what you can get done when you've made that commitment to be at home." Although we do not know if he actually leaves work at the time he says he does, or how much his progress has been hindered by time spent at home, the important thing here is that he describes himself as someone who puts family first. This is notable because this man *could* fit the model of the ideal scientist—he has a stay-at-home wife who takes care of practical family matters—but he would rather put time limits on his work so that he can spend time with his son.

Scientists who put family first often feel "interrupted" or "slowed down" at work as a result of their decision, and this can sometimes lead to professional consequences. It must be noted, however, that even though these scientists make the decision to put family first, they do not necessarily fully accept or agree with the professional costs associated with this choice; rather, they have decided that prioritizing their family is important enough to endure such professional consequences, and they acknowledge this fact. As one physicist put it, she has "made a decision to just go home every day kind of early [*laughs*], and if that will keep me from getting tenure, then I won't get tenure. I can't really care about it that much. So, I've made a decision to put as much time as I possibly can into the home life."[58]

Many scientists mention a loss of research productivity as a result of the decision to spend time with their families, but others focus on how the desire to spend more time at home has resulted in less time dedicated to broader university service rather than to research.[59] One assistant professor of physics in her late thirties is raising two young sons, aged one and three, with her husband, a physicist in a faculty position at a nearby university. Both are now working to secure tenure.[60] When she completed her postdoctoral fellowship, she received ten faculty job offers—an impressive feat that is a testament to her talent and potential—and she has been highly successful in her career. Yet the hours she spends at work are constrained due to child care responsibilities, so she must severely restrict the time she spends teaching, performing university service, or engaging in professional leadership in her disciplinary associations. As she explained: "I leave as *soon* [her emphasis] as I can, and I cut out all activities that are not absolutely essential to my research program—you know, maintain a program that's successful—and get [my children] as soon as I can so that I can spend at least part of the afternoon with them."

As her experience illustrates, the structure of academic science can be its own worst enemy. When a scientist decides to put family first in a system that does not support investment in family life, it is not only the scientist who might suffer professional consequences; universities often also lose out on a scientist's potential contribution to the institution.

For other scientists, putting family first involves financial and personal sacrifices, due to the amount of money and time needed to secure high-quality, full-time care for young children. One full professor of biology, whose husband is a professor in the same department and who has two daughters, now ten and thirteen, recalled:

> We lived in a very small house—like 1,100 square feet—with four of us because we needed money to pay [for child care]. You know, until our kids were in kindergarten, we had a full-time nanny, and then after that, it was part-time, but, you know, you're paying someone a salary, and that's a lot of money. So only at the point when the nanny went part-time could we afford to move into a larger house [*laughs*]. But, so I feel like that was a sacrifice. But my husband and I knew this was the only way we could manage for both of us to have this job and have kids and do it in the least stressful way.[61]

A married associate professor of physics who is the primary breadwinner for her family said that when she moved to her current university, her pay "went up by 50 percent [but] child care was a third of my salary . . . and that was with two kids. What if I had three kids?"[62]

Besides child care being costly, finding quality child care can take a good deal of time and energy. Another physicist said that finding quality day care is the "most critical point" for her.[63] She continued:

> I have to say that [my university] did a *bad* thing. They [do] have a day care center, which is extremely bad. They have a huge teacher turnover. They outsourced it to a company—a for-profit company—which has been just horrible. . . . It's a very, very important thing for people with young children. And that [the university] just took the best offer or the cheapest option or something like that instead of making sure that it's very high quality . . . [*trails off momentarily*] I mean, it just seems to me like an obvious thing.

This physicist and her husband found community day care for their two sons, and she is satisfied with the "continuity of care" it offers. But in her view, her university fails to structurally meet the child care needs of its faculty, and putting family first meant that she had to do extra work to find acceptable child care, a severe drain on her energy and time.

For some scientists, the decision to put family first arises only after earlier arrangements have harmed the family dynamic. Relatively few scientists are divorced when compared with the national average of about 50 percent, yet roughly half of the scientists who have divorced attribute the divorce to their science career (table 4.2).

TABLE 4.2. Percentage of Divorced Academic Scientists, by Gender and Career Stage*

	Graduate Students	Post-doctoral Fellows	Assistant Professors	Associate Professors	Full Professors
Men					
Divorced	1.0	3.7	8.9	16.5	22.9
Divorced due to science career	1.0	1.3	5.8	8.5	9.5
Fewer children than wished due to science career	20.3	39.0	35.4	27.6	13.9
Women					
Divorced	1.7	4.0	15.2	15.6	31.0
Divorced due to science career	1.4	2.5	10.6	9.5	15.0
Fewer children than wished due to science career	39.4	55.4	60.0	46.8	33.0

*Totals not reported because the number of persons responding to each question differs. There is attrition between responding to whether one has children and whether one has had fewer children than wished.

One tenured astronomer in his late thirties believes that working long hours seven days a week was one factor that contributed to his divorce from his first wife.[64] Now remarried to another academic scientist, he prioritizes his family above his work. As he stated:

> [My wife] is not tenured, so I know exactly the kind of pressure that she's going [through] and I know that there's no other choice [than] for me to do certain things. And [now] I have more time that I spend with my children. I take my daughter after school. We do more activities. But that is a big challenge, and that is something that I guess I regret. I guess I regret that I didn't realize earlier [with my older children].

As he once told his adolescent daughter: "The fact that I come to pick you up after school every day might means there's one paper less that I'm writing or reading, but I think that this is worth it."

For others, the decision to put family first emerges as their children grow older and they feel the pressure of family time running out. A tenured biologist in her midforties, whose husband is a professor in the same department, initially resented that her young son took time away from her career.[65] Now that he is entering elementary school, her attitude has completely changed. She said their relationship "has gotten stronger to where I would just rather be with him. I don't want to lose that time. Now I look at it in a different way."

Work Is More Important

While there were scientists who told us stories about how they place family before work, other scientists described how, for them, work comes first, and this shapes the narrative of their lives. Some put work first by establishing that their primary job is science, and their spouse must take the lead on family responsibilities. Generally, the spouse is a nonscientist who stays home full-time or works in a more limited capacity or a less prestigious field. An assistant professor of physics said his wife, who works as a financial specialist, shoulders the majority of the child care responsibilities for their two young children, while he makes work his first priority.[66] She "certainly is very understanding of the fact that one has to pursue tenure and one has to have these goals and this and that, and of course she's taking most of the toll," he explained.

It is not only male scientists who prioritize work above all else. One biologist with tenure described how she puts work first. "You have to unwrap the little hands around you in the morning when you drop them at day care," she said, "and then you have to, you know, not volunteer for things, and not do things."[67]

A friendly and upbeat associate professor of biology in her early forties who has carved out a highly successful science career said she has "always had sort of a turbulent personal life," including going through a divorce from her college sweetheart while in graduate school.[68] Of the divorce she said: "It didn't actually come down to this, but it was clear to me even at the time that if I had to make a choice between having the kind of science career that I wanted or being able to stay with him, it was just not even going to be a contest." Her career as a scientist "was a much more fundamental part of my identity than that relationship was," she said, "and I guess arguably than any of the relationships that I've had since then."

For some, putting work first means not having children, so that they don't have obligations that might "take away" from their work. One male professor of biology in his late fifties explained his decision to remain child-free this way:

> [The] timing is really difficult because having gone into the sciences the way that I did and enjoying it so much might have influenced not having children. Had I had children, whether or not I would have done as much in the sciences as I am currently doing, I can't guess, but I suspect no. In fact, in reflecting on this now, my wife has a number of times said to me—you know it's always her claim and she's probably right—if my first love is my science and if we had children, I wouldn't be able to do anywhere near as much as I do. I think she's right.[69]

And one physicist made it very clear that he chose not to have children because he wanted to be able to devote all his time to science.[70] In his words: "To be a successful scientist, it just takes so much of my time. I wouldn't be able to have children and also [be a scientist]. If I had a nine-to-five job, I could [have children]. . . . [Yet,] basically, I'm just kind of monomaniacally pursuing science."

For others, putting work first is not a long-term strategy but a temporary measure that is required when a major hurdle is approaching at work, such as meeting a grant proposal deadline or obtaining tenure. A number of scientists described prioritizing tenure above all else. Evan, who waited until he was close to being granted tenure to start a family, recalled:

> I worried like crazy for the first few years about tenure; [it] dominated my life, which it does for everybody. . . . It was really hard on my marriage because whenever there was stuff to do with the [younger kid], things that happened before he was two years old, I'd be like, "Sorry, can't do it, I got to work on this, I need to get tenure."[71]

Why Similarities between Men and Women Matter

These findings of similarities between men and women matter because they represent a shift in academic science that universities must address. The demographic that established and embodied the ideal scientist is gone. Although some scientists still prioritize work above everything else—devoting to it all their passion and time—many mid-career academic scientists, both male and female, want both a career and a family, and they are willing to sacrifice advancement, prestige, or sleep to get it.[72]

Here is why this is important for universities to recognize: happiness outside of work is strongly correlated with work satisfaction. Findings from our survey reveal that among both men and women in academic science, those who are more satisfied with their personal lives are 60 percent more likely to report being satisfied with their careers.[73] And what predicts personal life satisfaction for faculty members? Among the strongest influences are career satisfaction, being married, and whether family size goals have been met. Whether academic science likes it or not, the personal and professional lives of its faculty are intertwined. And research shows that people who feel happier at work simply do better work and do better science.

Yet universities are not currently providing adequate resources to support high-level academic scientists who are married with children.

Instead, these scientists often are met with a structure and culture that still exalt the ideal scientist of a bygone era. They often are penalized and stigmatized. So while these senior scientists appear to "have it all"—tenured positions at top research universities, spouses and kids—they are not thriving and flourishing. Rather, they are merely surviving a controlled crash.

5

When the Ideal Scientist Meets the Ideal Mother

OK, if you're married, do you take off your ring when you go for a job interview? Or do you put it on? The . . . lore is that with a man, you put it on because it shows that you are in a stable relationship. With a woman, you take it off because they're afraid you're going to get pregnant.
—Female graduate student in physics, late twenties[1]

I think a lot of people [in science] are saying, "When are you going to start a family?" Because they basically think, "OK, she's going to get pregnant. And she's not going to have time for this. . . . And she won't be able to put in extra hours. And she's going to be worrying about the baby. So her career is going to be stalled." And I think that's the main discrimination issue [in science]. Especially when they look at me and I am a woman. And they are like, "All right, do you want a family?" [And] yes I do!
—Female biologist who left science to pursue university administration, early thirties[2]

Carolyn, the professor of biology who juggles two children with her successful science career, encourages other women to join her lab, and yet she finds that she is not able to keep young women from leaving it—and science altogether—after they have children. Lately, this has made it difficult for Carolyn to sustain her research as fully as she would like. When men leave academic science, they tend to go to more lucrative careers in industry, she pointed out, but the women Carolyn sees leaving academic science often take less demanding jobs or stay home to care for their children full-time. She also observed that motherhood can function as an "out"—an escape from science—something she has seen among some of the young women in her lab. Many of the female students who leave "look at me and say, 'I don't want to live like you,'" she said. According to Carolyn, they don't see the value and purpose of a life of science alongside mothering. She continued: "I want to say, 'Oh my god, you are going to be insane. Give yourself five years. Your kids are going to be in school and what are you going to do?'" She finds it "very depressing" and asked: "Are they better off in a lab where there is not so much room [to have children]?"

In response to calls by the NSF, the National Academy of Sciences, and other national science bodies to be concerned about how many young scientists leave academic research careers, many social scientists have looked at why women leak from the academic science pipeline at higher rates than men.[3] Women still shoulder the majority of family responsibilities, even when they hold professional jobs or are in dual-career marriages, and science is a time-demanding profession that allows for few responsibilities outside of work. Thus, some argue that gender disparities in the academic sciences are directly linked to work-family conflict for women.[4]

We believe that the retention of women is important to the success and progress of science and the quality and diversity of research. Therefore, it is important to uncover why fully qualified women leave science at higher rates than men.

Our survey results show some of the unique ways that work-family conflict affects female scientists. Female scientists have fewer children than their male colleagues,[5] and nearly twice as many women as men (about 45 percent vs. about 25 percent) report having fewer children than desired because they pursued a science career (table 5.1).[6]

Furthermore, a higher proportion of female scientists than male scientists say they are dissatisfied with their roles as faculty members, and our interviews with these scientists reveal that some of this dissatisfaction stems from responsibilities in the home.[7] At elite U.S. research universities, both male and female scientists without children work about sixty hours a week, and scientist parents do work fewer hours.[8] Yet we found that at these universities, women biologists and physicists with children *do not* work fewer hours than men with children—both work about fifty-five hours a week.[9] Yet it is likely that these women spend

TABLE 5.1. Scientists' Number of Children and Those Who Want More*

	Graduate Students	Post-doctoral Fellows	Assistant Professors	Associate Professors	Full Professors
Men					
Number of children	0.11	0.53	1.00	1.55	1.95
Fewer children than wished due to science career (%)	20.3	39.0	35.4	27.6	13.9
Women					
Number of children	0.07	0.26	0.81	1.27	1.48
Fewer children than wished due to science career (%)	39.4	55.4	60.0	46.8	33.0

*Totals not reported because the number of persons responding to each question differs. There is attrition between responding to whether one has children and whether one has had fewer than wished.

more time taking care of home and family responsibilities than their male counterparts do.

When we analyzed our survey results, comparing women at the same career stage, we found no difference in reports of discrimination between women who do and do not have children—yet both female and male scientists at all stages of the career course told us that women are more likely to suffer discrimination when they have children and try to maintain an academic science career at an elite research university. In their narratives many women pinpointed frustrating moments of both implicit and explicit discrimination—at the hands of advisers, colleagues, and the broader science community—as a result of their status as mothers. These women often attribute instances of discrimination to the perception held by some men (as well as some women) that being a mother equates to less chance of success in academic science. Notably, although many men in academic science perceive enormous work-family tension, scientist fathers seem much less likely to face discrimination based on their role as parents (table 5.2).

TABLE 5.2. Perceptions of Discrimination among Scientist Parents (%)*

	Graduate Students	Post-doctoral Fellows	Assistant Professors	Associate Professors	Full Professors
Scientist Fathers					
Has felt gender discrimination sometimes or often	3.6	6.7	3.0	4.2	4.7
Feels gender discrimination has hindered career	0	0	0	0	0.3
Scientist Mothers					
Has felt gender discrimination sometimes or often	5.3	27.3	28.2	42.2	47.4
Feels gender discrimination has hindered career	5.3	6.7	11.5	29.2	28.3

*Includes only respondents who reported having children.

When it comes to balancing academic science and parenthood, women and men still have distinctively different experiences. Some of these differences are biologically based; certainly, it is women who get pregnant, give birth, and breast-feed. Biological differences, however, are often reified in the way that structures are set up and instantiated in cultural meanings. Structures, such as department meeting times and promotion timelines that give preference to scientist fathers who have a stay-at-home wife, hurt young men who want to spend time with their children—but they hurt scientist mothers more. When structural factors and cultural forces (such as attitudes and perceptions of what good mothers and good fathers do) work together, profound sources of discrimination can emerge.

Structural and cultural factors also influence how scientist mothers create and adjust their identities. Women scientists usually do not feel supported at work when they have children. Moreover, they often neglect to seek the outside help they need (such as support from a partner or other caregivers for their children). In her book *The Cultural Contradictions of Motherhood*, sociologist Sharon Hays argues that women don't seek assistance because of constructs that tell them that the "ideal" mother does everything with no help from anyone, puts her child's needs above her own, and always acts against the societal norms of self-interest.[10] As Hays explains, the expectations for motherhood are at odds with the broader societal focus on individualistic market-centered gain. As a result, women tend to feel perpetually guilty for not spending enough time with their children; they feel lucky when their husbands *do* spend time with their children, but they do not expect it.[11] This guilt, stemming from societal expectations and cultural norms, influences both the parenting *and* the work of scientist mothers.

The Biological Factor

As one full professor of biology in her late forties pointed out, "The reality is, I'm the one who is going to be pregnant. I'm the one who's going to [*laughing*] deliver the baby . . . you know, you just can't change that."[12]

Although it is women who give birth and breast-feed, institutional structures designed to make the early stages of parenting easier for scientists often end up benefiting men more than women. For example, Jill, an associate professor of physics, pointed out how she thinks men in science tend to spend the time they "take off" after having a child.[13] According to her: "There are those men who took the paternity leave . . . and basically were in the office every day. It was like a sabbatical for them. . . . [A]t least in my experience, for women, it's just not physically possible for it to just be a sabbatical when you have a kid; for men, it is."

An associate professor of biology, who is married to another academic scientist, told us that the experience of being a mother "is certainly different" from the experience of being a father.[14] Most of the time, she and her husband successfully split child care responsibilities, she said, but she admitted that she has more responsibilities at home than her husband does, and this was especially the case when their children were very young. When the children were little, she said, her husband had no problem traveling, but she "didn't like leaving the kids." As a woman, she explained, "I did feel, sort of, a biologically derived [sense of being] more responsible for the kids."

Pregnancy

On average, women in the United States have about two children,[15] and they live about eighty-one years,[16] which means they are pregnant for less than 2 percent of their lifetime. Statistically, the female biologists and physicists who responded to our survey have one child on average, yet the impact pregnancy had on their science careers spanned much longer than nine months.

We found that only rarely does being pregnant have a direct impact on women's scientific work. In one of the very few instances that came up in our interviews with biologists and physicists, a biology postdoctoral fellow in her early thirties explained how being pregnant changed the kind of work she could do: "I used to love working in the lab with the chemicals and things, [but] when I was pregnant, I couldn't do some of the things in the lab that I would have otherwise been doing because I couldn't work with those kind of chemicals."[17]

Women did note, however, that being pregnant during a job interview is a huge detriment to being hired. When Elaine asked a thirty-one-year-old postdoctoral fellow to share any experience of discrimination in science, she immediately responded, "I've heard stories of people not getting interviews or jobs because they're visibly pregnant on an interview."[18] She also recalled the experience of a friend who, during a difficult pregnancy, received little support at work:

> One of my former colleagues here, a postdoc, when I got here, was pregnant . . . and she received a lot of discrimination about that. . . . [P]eople said things to me behind her back all the time . . . like her boss said some things that I thought were completely outrageous, and about, you know, she should be working harder.

Breast-feeding

More often than discussing the impact of pregnancy on their work, female scientists talked about how biological differences influenced parenting responsibilities after the birth of a child. Breast-feeding was a particularly hot topic. Elaine met Joanne, an assistant professor of biology in her early thirties with a two-month-old baby, in Joanne's office. Elaine noticed a recliner with a blue knit throw on it and quickly thought it might be a good chair for nursing an infant.[19] Having just had her own baby six months earlier, she also wondered, would someone who hadn't just had a baby be surprised by her observation?

In the United States, the push to breast-feed for a longer period is promoted by the health care profession as a way to enhance a baby's and mother's health.[20] More recently, some women's studies scholars have added a new perspective. According to one scholar, "Breastfeeding is a way to achieve so-called good mothering, the idealized notion of mothers as selfless and child-centered."[21] Interestingly, highly educated women are most likely to consider breast-feeding a positive and necessary part of bringing up a baby. On average, women who have at least a bachelor's degree are more likely to breast-feed their babies up to one year than are women who have not completed a bachelor's degree.

The scientists at the universities we studied are among the most educated women in the country, so it is likely these women know the health benefits of breast-feeding and are highly motivated to breast-feed their newborns. Yet, like many women in professional careers, scientists often have to travel for their work or for conferences—without their babies—making exclusive breast-feeding impossible. In addition, the scientist mothers we interviewed told us that rarely are there places on campus where they can pump breast milk. And on-campus day care centers, if they're available, are rarely close enough to women's offices to make feeding a baby during the workday feasible. Those who decided to continue breast-feeding, even without structures in place to support their efforts, negotiated personal, informal arrangements to make it possible, and these arrangements worked to varying degrees. One assistant professor of physics in her late thirties said she nurses her son in her office and hopes "that no one will open the door, because I can't lock it."[22]

Breast-feeding also affects scholarly productivity because of the sheer time commitment involved—and because some of that time can occur in the middle of the night. Exclusive breast-feeding can mean that it is *always* the mother who gets up with the baby to feed, and these late-night feedings can have a profound impact on the ability to accomplish work during the day. Exhaustion is not conducive to an elite career in academic science. When an associate professor of biology in her late forties reflected on the time she spent breast-feeding her son about a decade ago, she said she can hardly believe she made it through that period in her life:

> I would say the first three years were just crazy! I look back on it [and] I'm not even sure how I got through that in retrospect. . . . There were times where I was up all night and I would breast-feed him every three hours while I was writing a grant. I mean, I'd write my grants, he'd cry, breast-feed him, put him back down, write my grant [*laughs*]. I've done stuff like that.[23]

One of the scientists we talked with told us about her friend, a scientist mother who has to leave her lab every hour to pump. "And it's actually a lot more inconvenient than it sounds," the biologist telling the story said with a laugh, "because she has to do experiments. And so she actually can't work as much as she did before, because of the pumping."[24]

Part of what makes things harder for scientist mothers than scientist fathers, as Joanne succinctly put it, is that "if you're a female, you have to actually do the being pregnant and producing milk and all that sort of stuff, so it's impossible for child rearing to be completely egalitarian. . . . I have to be more engaged in the process than a male counterpart would have to be necessarily."

Research Is in Competition with Childbirth

Looking back over the course of her career, an associate professor of biology told us:

> After I got tenure and maybe a few months after that, I finally felt like this, "Whew I can finally breathe." And so that's when we started thinking about [having kids]. . . . I wish we would have started thinking about it before . . . everything up until that point in my life has sort of been, five years in PhD, three years in postdoc, you know then you are an assistant professor, then you get tenure, and it's sort of been like by the book. . . . [W]e have talked about if things don't work out, maybe adopt-

> ing. It seems like whatever road we're facing now, I think is going to be long and emotionally difficult.[25]

Given the reality of the childbearing years, the competition between the tenure clock and the *biological* clock is especially acute for women. This competition affects not only if and when women have children but also how hard they work before they have children, fearing how much harder it will be to get work done after a baby is born. When we spoke with a thirty-one-year-old postdoctoral fellow in biology who was seven months pregnant, she said she was working twelve-hour days, every day, and was "definitely productive, but I am fearing that that's going to go away once I have this kid [*laughs*]. . . . *I feel like my research is in a race against my fetus at this point*."[26]

Some female scientists choose to leave academic science when they have children, either for full-time mothering or for a career that seems more flexible and demands less time. Thinking about the women from her graduate school lab, one biologist in her early forties, who has an eight-year-old and an eleven-year-old, said:

> Going to the next level, that's where [they] drop off. . . . [W]omen tend to, for the most part, want to be a major part of the child's life, which takes up a lot of time that you could be maybe spending at work, or traveling, or—it's not so carefree, and I think that's probably a *huge* factor [her emphasis]. . . . [In graduate school] I was in a lab that was mostly women. I am the only one of the girls that I was with, that actually went on. The only one.[27]

Science Is Structured for the Scientist Father

What We Need Is a Wife

Joanne told us about a conversation she had with a male faculty member, the father of a one-year-old child.[28] They were discussing child care strategies, she said, when she discovered that he "doesn't really have an understanding of what might be involved when you have two people working because his wife is taking care of the child."

As we have seen, the structure of academic science is still best suited to a male scientist who has a stay-at-home wife. A forty-two-year-old associate professor of biology, who is in a commuter marriage (her husband lives several states away from where her university is located) and has two children, aged one and five, said that "for the majority of my [older] male colleagues, their wives have either part-time jobs or are home with their kids. And that makes it easier [*laughs*]. Obviously."[29] While some female scientists are married to men who work fewer hours than they do and have agreed to be the primary caregiver for the children, scientist mothers often do not have the support of a fully stay-at-home spouse. For example, Jill explained that her husband, who does not have an active career, "does not want the identity of the stay-at-home dad," an attitude she believes is common for men.[30] "There are definitely men who have the wife at home looking after the kids, and I guess that's it, that's the difference," she said. "There are men in astronomy who have the wife at home looking after the kids, and that's generally not true for women." In her case, she adds, she has "done *a lot* more child care than someone who has got a stay-at-home spouse would be doing."

Along the same lines, a professor of biology in her early fifties said:

> My observation is that many of my male colleagues have wives that stay at home, and that takes a tremendous amount of pressure off of them [*laughs*]. [The wives] really do manage the house and . . . totally schedule the children. You know, I block time in February to schedule summer camps. My male colleagues are not doing that. I volunteered a half day in my children's school for many years. I don't see my male colleagues doing that [*laughs*]. So I think that they are probably spending significantly less time . . . doing the work of being a parent.[31]

As a result, a number of female scientists said that, due to family demands, they simply could not work the same hours as their male colleagues—even though, as noted earlier, women with children actually report working the *same* number of hours as men with children.[32] As we also noted earlier, because a greater share of home and family responsibilities tend to fall on women's shoulders, it is often harder for them to make contributions to science outside of their primary work role and university setting, particularly when travel is involved. As a full professor of biology and mother of three noted: "Child care has been hard, and then just getting everything done is challenging. . . . I've chosen not to travel very much . . . about a third as much as I could. . . . And I think that does impact, certainly your national reputation and your ability to form collaborations."[33]

Hilary, a biology professor in her midfifties, has two teenage boys she raised as a single mother.[34] When her kids were growing up, she was one of only a few women in her department, and the *only* faculty member with children who did not have a spouse at home. "All of my colleagues here, their wives either did not work or went to half-time positions," she said. "So, all of them, their wives took care of everything, right? . . . So their wives could handle everything." Her department colleagues were "completely clueless" about the struggles that came along with being a single mother in science, she remembers, such as paying out of pocket for babysitters every time she was asked to host a job candidate or graduate student for dinner.

When she was up for tenure, Hilary even hid the fact that she had two small sons from the review board, at the suggestion of her dean. She recalled:

> After the chairs in the School of Science voted to give me tenure, he said to them: "Guess what, you just voted to give this woman tenure and she has two kids." . . . [T]hey had voted without knowing that based on my record, right? So . . . the fact that that happened really changed things for women [at my university]. So the fact that the dean felt that it had to be a secret because if it was known, all of his colleagues would have voted against me [because I was a woman with children] with the same academic record.

Although academic science is more accepting of scientist mothers today than when Hilary was going through the tenure process, she believes that balancing work and parenting is still easier for scientist fathers. She elaborated:

> My generation, the assumption was you wouldn't have children . . . over a ten-year window. There was a real shift to, now, it's expected that women will have kids. In terms of whether it's changed enough that there is an expectation that men will be equally involved in sort of managing the children and managing the home . . . I think practically that almost never played out. You know, it's really the women who [are] taking care of things.

Cultural Interpretations

Despite dramatic changes in the labor force and family structure over the past forty years, there is still a cultural expectation that wives are responsible for household activities and husbands act as breadwinners for their families.[35] Men may value time with family and help with child care, but they are not yet culturally expected to care for household activities. Scientist mothers, on the other hand, are expected to fulfill the obligations of two full-time roles. Academic science expects them to be ideal scientists, working long hours and devoting themselves fully to their work, while at the same time they are culturally expected to be ideal mothers, devoting themselves fully to their children. The expectation that women will be full-time mothers, regardless of their participation in the labor market, springs from the "ideology of intensive mothering."[36] This form of mothering is so intense, all-encompassing, and selfless—requiring women to disburse time, energy, and money into raising a child in a totally altruistic way—that gender scholar Sharon Hays has argued it is impossible to achieve, even for a woman who stays home full-time with her children and has no outside pursuits.

Jill described the self-inflicted pressure she feels to be an ideal mother, even though she has a husband who is willing to be the primary caregiver for their children:

> I would say the challenge in the first couple of years was myself. Because I found once I was going back to work, I was trying to go to work and then come home and take over from him in the evenings. . . . Of course I found that completely draining to, in effect, be doing two jobs, and eventually I realized that was my problem, not his problem. . . . I was trying to make up for things where I didn't need to make up for them—so that's what I was meaning when I was saying myself as part of the challenge. How I have been socialized is part of the challenge.[37]

"Society" Expects More from Women as Parents Than Men

Because the ideology of intensive mothering pervades our cultural landscape, societal institutions such as schools, doctor's offices, day care centers, religious organizations, and even other families expect women to fulfill more of the family caregiving role than men. As an assistant professor of biology put it, "There's a certain extent to which moms are sort of called on to play a larger role in child rearing than dads are."[38] Women are "called on" both literally—by schools and sports camps, for example, who always put them first on the list of parents to call—and metaphorically by broader society to selflessly attend to their children. This "calling"—the duty to be the altruistic mother—makes it extremely difficult for female scientists at elite research universities to balance parenting with the work that is required and expected of them.

A senior professor of biology in her late forties, who is married to another academic and has preteen children, explained:

> I remember at certain points feeling like, "OK, to get this grant done I have to be superwoman right now." But then it got to be a point where I am superwoman almost all the time [*laughs*]. It gets kind of exhausting after a while. And then you realize you can't expect all women to do this. My male colleagues don't have to be *superman*! You know, I have to be superwoman because I have kids. I end up dealing with anything having to do with the kids, basically their whole social schedules, the doctor appointments. You know, everything—music lessons, sports, filling all those forms out. It all comes down to me, and it's a lot of work, and you just can't expect every *woman* to be willing to do that, and men don't have to. . . . [I]t's clear why there's a problem, but I don't know what the solution is.[39]

Women Are "Lucky" and Men "Sacrifice"

Male and female scientists frame their contributions to family life in different ways. Both male and female scientists tend to label household management and child care as primarily female tasks. Even though younger men in science seem to value time with family more than earlier generations of male scientists did, family responsibilities among scientists continue to reflect traditional gender norms. As Laurie, the biology professor in her late forties we met in chapter 4, explained:

> I think women come to work knowing that they have to get everything done and there is a deadline, and you've got to get it done and get out of here. . . . My male colleagues, they can be here all night and all day, and

> they don't have to go home and worry about the laundry and whether the dogs are let out, and those are just not things [*trails off*]. Now, granted, I could make my husband maybe do that more, but it wasn't part of our relationship, and you could say that's my fault, but I see that a lot in my friends who are women like me who have husbands that are also professionals, that we [the women] do everything.[40]

We found that men describe their family contributions as sacrifices, whereas women emphasize how lucky they are if their partner contributes equally to child-rearing tasks. Women also stressed feeling lucky if they were married to a man who was willing to place family needs before his ideal career conditions in order to help his wife succeed in science. Yet these men often stress their particularly accommodating role. There remains an underlying belief that in dual-career couples, the man's career should come first.

One associate professor of biology in her late thirties, who does not yet have children because she waited until after she gained tenure to try, said she feels "lucky" that her husband, who is currently working toward his doctorate, was twice willing to move with her for different university posts.[41] In her words, "He has been willing to just sort of let me have my career and he has had to compromise his ultimate goals." Ultimately, she said, "I felt lucky *that I* [emphasis hers] didn't have to follow him around."

Like many women, Carolyn expressed great appreciation for her husband, who commutes four hours each day, and she attributed her career success to the help and support he gave her.[42] "The only way that I could have been able to do it is my husband, period," Carolyn said. "I could never have done it myself; I don't think I have it in me."

Among the female scientists we interviewed who already had children or those who anticipated having children in the immediate future,, a little more than 34 percent used the word "lucky" in relation to their husband's or partner's willingness to help at home.[43] Not a single man used the word "lucky" to describe how he felt about the professional benefit he derived from his wife's work at home.

Women use the word "lucky" in diverse contexts, however. Female scientists who do not yet have children sometimes feel that they can pursue their careers because they anticipate their husbands will be willing to be very involved at home. A physicist who is a postdoctoral fellow admitted, "I don't quite know how [child care is] going to work. I've seen young faculty do it, and I feel very lucky with my husband; I think he'll be a true partner and will divide the task of child rearing."[44] In other words, she feels lucky that she can even *consider* the possibility of being a mother because her husband has indicated he will help at home. Other women simply feel lucky if they have a husband who does not ask them to sacrifice their career for his, even if child care is not evenly split. One biologist who is an associate professor said that although she and her husband are "really doing the same job . . . he's a full professor and I'm an associate professor . . . he probably does more of our finances, I do more of the child stuff . . . the family stuff. But . . . I'm really lucky. He's really, really supportive, and when we look for jobs, we really look at what would be best for both of us."[45]

In response to these reflections, we wonder why these women consider themselves "lucky" when they are in relationships with men who contribute to child care or support their wife's career. We believe it is because a family structure in which there is a male breadwinner and a female caregiver is still the expected norm.[46] These women feel *lucky* that they are allowed to break from expectations. Here, perhaps, is a subliminal condemnation of the system itself: a woman is lucky to have an exit or escape from it. Notably, these women also perceive themselves as exceptions to the rule, the uncommon minority. They are lucky to break away from what they perceive to be the norm for women: operation within a structural economic system where men are breadwinners and a cultural landscape where women are characterized as nurturing and domestic to the exclusion of other characterizations.

The Emotion Work of Mothers Who Are Scientists

An associate professor of biology in her late fifties mused that being a mother and a scientist is not just about societal norms that pressure women to spend more time engaged in child care activities, but also about the emotion norms of how a scientist perceives herself, a condition that is fueled by but even harder to address than societal norms. She explained:

> Even now with my kids are as old as they are . . . when issues come up and somebody needs something—advice on something or whatever—it's always me that sort of handles the kid things. . . . *For me it was a bigger commitment not only of time, I think, but perhaps I was more emotionally invested.*[47]

Scholars use the term "emotion work" to refer to how an individual views which emotions are appropriate, which is in part constructed by the culture around her, in particular the specific social groups that she belongs to and what those groups tell her about her core identities.[48] For many women, pursuing an academic science career feels like a decision to minimize dedication to family, and these women speak extensively about the guilt they feel as they try to balance family with their work. This is something the men Elaine talked with almost never mentioned. Women's guilt comes from the expectation that they will be "full-time" mothers—at least in spirit—regardless of their participation in the labor market. For a woman in academic science, this guilt often gets incorporated into her perception of her shortcomings, as both a scientist and a mother. A physicist in her late thirties recalled that right after her pregnancy, it was difficult "just going through the hormones and the whole guilt trip of 'What am I doing here?'"[49] The guilt a woman feels for leaving her child with a caregiver while working, however, has more than simply biological roots. A professor of biology who waited until she had gained tenure to consider starting a family told me that she and her husband had to adopt a child because she "waited too long" and "couldn't have kids."[50] Right after they adopted their son, she too struggled to accommodate her work schedule, which had been her highest priority, to fit her son's needs. Now, though, she still regrets not spending adequate time with him. As she explained, "I'm mad if I have to lose that time [with him] because it just goes by so fast. And I wish I had had that insight when he was little, because he was so cute, and those were fun years." Clearly, her emotional struggle is similar to that of biological mothers and it has lasted well beyond the initial entry of a child into her family.

Although, as we saw in earlier chapters, men too expressed guilt for not spending enough time with their children, women scientists tended to express *more* guilt even though they also report spending *more* time with their children than do men. Several women shared what Carolyn calls "devastating" stories of being asked by their young children why they weren't picked up after school by their mother like other kids. Recall how Carolyn's daughter once challenged her to choose between her job as a scientist and her work as a mother.[51] As Carolyn told it:

> When my girls were little [the difficulties of being a scientist mother] took the form of being the only mom not to come and pick up my daughter after school. She had to go to day care on campus. . . . She was always in day care growing up, but when she finally got into the school system, there are a lot of moms that don't work, in fact most of them don't, and so . . . suddenly she realized all these other moms are coming to get their daughters. "Well don't you love me mom? Don't you love me more than your job?" [she said once].

A biologist in her midforties shared a similar story: "[My son] said, 'Well, why do you have to work? . . . [W]hy can't you be like so-and-so's mom, and be home?'"[52]

An associate professor of biology whose husband is also an academic biologist spoke at length about raising her two young sons.[53] She came to tears when discussing the tension she feels between love for her career and her greater love for her children. "I would love to be more involved with their school. I would love to have more time . . . and I love to be invited to these meetings and stuff, but then it's so hard—you know," she said. "I feel like I don't have time and they are growing up fast."

Employing a nanny or finding other caregivers for their children can also lead to fraught emotions for female scientists, as children who spend more time with their caregivers than their mothers can start to show a preference for their caregivers. Evan, an associate professor of biology in his late forties we met in the last chapter, explained the emotional "trauma" that his wife, also an academic, went through with their two small children: "The kids were closer to the nanny than they were to her, and when something happened, they would cry for the nanny. Her heart would break and then, you know, [she'd say,] 'My God, my kids love my nanny more than they love me.'"[54]

Most parents who hire caregivers to help them tend to their children sometimes experience guilt over not fulfilling the traditional parental roles. Women who hire caregivers also feel the additional guilt of not living up to the "ideology of intensive mothering," however unrealistic it may be, and this guilt can lead to further stress. Women with a heightened sense of responsibility toward their families often try their best to balance work with family life, though it can come with a professional cost.

An associate professor of biology in her midforties described the consequences of her emotional stress this way:

> I was not enjoying my work. . . . I'd be writing grants that I didn't think I was going to get. I didn't know what was going to happen—I was worrying about how to keep the lab going. And then at home I had these adorable little boys that are saying "Stay home with me, Mommy!" And I was really asking myself, "Why am I doing this?" . . . And I think it's really hard to do everything, and it's really hard to have kids.[55]

She recalled a weekday when she decided to miss work so she could attend her son's swim class, a decision she attributes to the "mom factor." Her husband felt fine skipping the class because it took place on a workday; his response was, "Oh, well, so we can't go." But thinking about her son's emotions, as well as how other parents might respond to her not being there, motivated her to go. She remembers thinking, "You know, he's going to be sad. The other parents are going to be there." She would feel responsible for her son's sadness, and so she felt compelled to perform emotional "labor" to avoid this reaction. So "I took my work and I sat in the corner of summer camp. I found a quiet place . . . [and] I did all my e-mails until it was time and then I went to his swim thing," she recalled. Not surprisingly, she said, "My son was delighted." "I mean, I could also have just not gone," she concluded, "but as a mom, I couldn't, you know?" In her view, attending events like swim class is an essential part of her "job description" as a mom, and she feels compelled to complete that duty even if it interferes with her work as a scientist.

The sense that guilt goes along with being a scientist mother is so pervasive that some women who plan to have children choose to exit science altogether. The woman quoted at the beginning of this chapter left academia in part because she worried that the guilt over leaving her future child would be more than she could handle.[56] "I think," she said, "the woman always feels huge guilt for leaving the baby, you know?"

Mother Discrimination

Many of the women interviewed said that overt discrimination against mothers is real, and there is clearly a sense in academic science that being a mother is detrimental to a science career.

"A Mommy Kind of Person"

Joanne told Elaine that if a scientist mother's performance at work is seen as not living up to standards associated with the ideal scientist, it is often explicitly and automatically connected to her status as a mother.[57] She said her colleagues talk about one female scientist who had a baby and complain, "'Oh, after she had the kid, she doesn't come to faculty meetings anymore.' Well, I mean, it's bad that she doesn't come to faculty meetings anymore, but like blaming someone's lack of engagement on having a child, while there are other faculty members who are not engaged and [their colleagues] just don't care." As Joanne sees it, her colleagues' reaction implies that it is acceptable to miss faculty meetings for almost any reason, except being a mother. She emphasized that "you don't want to be too much of a *mommy kind of person* in this career. You know, you don't want to give off the vibe that you just want to have lots of children. I think everyone would frown at you and think you weren't very serious." In her view, if a woman is known to have a child—or, worse, to relish motherhood too much—her seriousness as a professional will immediately be discounted.

Joanne was not alone in mentioning these concerns. Women often discussed decisions regarding children in terms of how these choices would influence senior men's (and sometimes senior women's) judgments about how serious these women were about their careers.

"At Least It's Not as Hard as It Used to Be"

The sense that being a scientist mother is a particularly challenging experience pervaded many interviews, yet the narratives that mothers shared were strongly influenced by their age. Older women who had experienced extreme forms of discrimination in academic science described responding in extreme ways. Carolyn hid her infant "in the drawer," and Hilary hid her children's existence throughout the tenure process. Hilary said that, at the time, she had heard of only a small handful of women at her institution who had started a family before receiving tenure. As she saw it,

> I just sort of had to do it and then prove to them that it was possible, right? And then that made it possible, I think, for subsequent women to have children and not be disregarded as a professional person. And now people even have . . . maternity leave, right? . . . People can even take time off or even stop their tenure [clock] for a year, so things have really turned around.

A full professor of physics in her early sixties said, "I would have wanted my husband to participate more. . . . I could've used more help. . . . [But] that's . . . something I see changing. . . . [T]he women postdocs [and] the graduate students that have had children now, I see their husbands really shouldering more of the burden and helping out."[58] The shift is obvious to this older cohort of women: things are looking up for scientist mothers.

Despite the perception among some senior female scientists that the experience of being a scientist mother is improving and discrimination is declining, younger women still perceive subtle or not-so-subtle forms of discrimination for being a mother or wanting to be a mother. One woman we interviewed, a thirty-one-year-old biology postdoctoral fellow, asserted, "There's just so many things about family life that I feel like universities are not catching up to."[59] Consequently, she admitted, "My goals for my career have changed dramatically in the last six months, and a lot of it has to do with [*long pause*] balance between family life and work." She said that when she entered science—not long ago—she "thought that I was going to be in this generation that like, maybe, the people in the next generation after me would benefit from the change that my generation ushered in, in terms of changing the university system and how it treats professors and staff." She even felt, she said, "like, 'it's OK, I'm going to be the change.'" Yet, under the weight of academic pressures and the desire to have a family, she confessed, "I just decided that I'm actually not willing to be the change *because the change is not happening fast enough* [her emphasis]." She seems deflated as she drifts into her own thoughts. "I'm just not willing to live the life that I would need to," she said, "to be a part of that change and . . . [*sighs*]." She seems to indicate that she will leave academic science because of how it might impact her ability to have children.

When Elaine asked about experiences of discrimination in biology, one associate professor of biology shared a colleague's story.[60] When a graduate student in her program told the male director of graduate studies that she was pregnant, the director made "very inappropriate comments about the fact that she should not keep the baby" because "if she has this baby, you know, she's not likely to finish graduate school and so forth." Consequently, the graduate student is "giving the baby up for adoption."

Is It Worse in Physics?

Women have now entered the highest ranks of tenured faculty positions in biology: about 30 percent of associate professors and 19 percent of full professors are women. In physics, however, only 19 percent of associate professors and 8 percent of full professors are women. The work of scholars who examine how the representation of women and men within an organization can influence work experiences is relevant when we compare the experiences of scientist mothers in physics with the experiences of those in biology. For example, in their respective classic works, sociologist Judith Blau and business scholar Rosabeth Moss Kanter discuss how social contact between dominant and subordinate groups in an organization influences group relations, and they predict that increasing social contact between majority and minority groups will reduce animosity.[61] In contrast, in his seminal work on minority group relations, sociologist Hubert Blalock argues that regardless of the level of social interaction, dominant groups (e.g., men) will be threatened by the increasing size of socially subordinate groups (e.g., women).[62]

Sociologists have found that women in male-dominated occupations perceive lower levels of support than do women in sex-integrated occupations, and conversely, men in female-dominated occupations perceive relatively high levels of support. They argue that individuals are influenced by perceptions of what constitutes an appropriate worker for a given job, and these perceptions influence feelings of support in the workplace.[63] In academic science—and particularly in physics, where there are far fewer women than in biology—women should perceive less support at work than men, since science has traditionally been a male-typed occupation. Additionally, based on the dominant cultural model, men will see themselves as having a primary identity as a worker and, at best, a secondary identity as a caregiver.[64]

We find that the experience of being a mother in physics is quite different from the experience of being a mother in biology, exemplifying the ways in which the cultural norms of a department or discipline affect the lived experiences of individuals. Our survey results show that male physicists consistently report higher levels of support from their departments than do male biologists. The opposite is true among women: female physicists generally report lower levels of departmental support than do women in biology (table 5.3).

TABLE 5.3. Perceptions of Department Support among Scientists (%)

Department Support	Graduate Students	Postdoctoral Fellows	Assistant Professors	Associate Professors	Full Professors
Men					
Biology	91.4	92.9	91.9	82.6	86.1
Physics	92.6	93.9	92.5	91.6	91.6
Women					
Biology	91.9	92.3	84.1	64.7	85.7
Physics	88.0	87.1	71.1	73.3	70.4
Total	**684**	**504**	**446**	**326**	**543**

A twenty-six-year-old physics graduate student nonchalantly explained the cultural norm in her discipline:

> The kind of standard model [*a play on the physics*] for what it looks like to have work [and] life balanced if you're a woman in the field is that you maybe have one child or maybe you don't have any [*laughs*] and then that child, unless you wait until you're thirty-eight and have tenure, that child goes into day care. You know, full-time day care at the age of six months and you're still working twelve-hour days.[65]

An assistant professor of physics was even more blunt: "Maybe what it takes for a woman to make it in physics is to be able to hand off her kid at eight weeks flat, and then go back to work eight to five, until the day care center closes."[66]

A young physicist who just completed her PhD seems to have reflected a great deal on issues of family and gender, as well as institutional discrimination, and had many interesting observations and insights about these issues.[67] She got married a year ago, and her husband recently completed his PhD in astronomy. She is currently at a stage in life when her career goals and desire to have children seem in conflict, and she feels like she has to choose between the two. She said she definitely wants to finish her degree but is not sure that she is willing to go through the next steps needed to stay in the field, largely due to family considerations. She said that concerns about whether it is possible to raise a family while being a physicist, as well as concerns about the suitability of her particular skills to a career in academic science, decrease her motivation to work through tough problems. Concerns about the *possibility* of raising a family are so salient for this young physicist that they are actually impacting her productivity—even though she does not yet have children! When asked about challenges she has faced in her career, she immediately responded that the biggest challenge is how to have children and stay in science. She has not seen models of how to have a family and pursue an academic science career, and she is particularly concerned about child care. Family, she said, will be a large factor in her decision about whether or not to pursue academic science.

Several scientists in both biology and physics argued that physics is an especially labor-intensive and demanding field and suggested that women may be more likely to leave physics than biology because of their perception that the discipline places greater restrictions on family life. Women may think that physics departments, in particular, desire scientists who are willing to sacrifice family responsibilities; as a result, women may choose to pursue a career in a discipline perceived as more flexible for family choices. A female biology professor suggested that in physics "women feel like it's too hard to . . . wear all of these hats. And so they've opted out." A female associate professor of physics said that the difficulty of balancing family demands and a physics career is "not going to be solved until we figure out how to help mothers figure out how to do the career and the kid thing."

Although these scientists argued that it might be harder for women in physics than women in biology to balance family life and career, the survey data demonstrate that female scientists in biology work approximately the same number of hours per week as female scientists in physics. Perhaps balancing work and family is not actually harder in physics, but the *perception* persists that being a physicist causes greater work-family tension than being a biologist. And, as sociologists, we know that what people believe is real—even if only in their imaginations—they act on as real.

When Scientists Are Too Good at Being Mothers

Scholars have highlighted the collective undervaluation of non-economically "rational" behavior in modern society.[68] Motherhood, however, as conceived in the "ideology of intensive mothering," is based on models of selflessness, nurturing, and pursuing actions outside of self-interest that are in complete opposition to *Homo economicus*—the idea, common in modern economic analysis, that humans are primarily rational and self-interested beings who struggle for profit and individual gain in both the public and the private sphere.[69] As a result, workplace behaviors that are interpreted as too "nurturing" or "motherly" can be a source of conflict, and a few of the women we talked with shared particularly poignant stories about how this played out in academic science.

An associate professor of biology told us that others have criticized her because, in her words, "I wasn't running my lab the right way because I was being *too nurturing* of my students."[70] In other words, she experiences disapproval from other scientists because she exudes a feminized, "mother-like" quality in her workplace.

Other mothers Elaine interviewed appeared not to act out of individualistic self-interest—the noted norm of the workplace—but out of genuine concern for the well-being of others, especially those with lower social status or less power. As Sharon Hays indicates, such behavior is well within the domain of the ideology of intensive mothering, but it is not necessarily compatible with the workplace.

For example, a forty-six-year-old associate professor of biology demonstrates how "motherly" behavior and consideration for the welfare of others can be a hidden detriment to a woman's career.[71] She said she "was writing grants all the time—I wasn't getting them. My lab was shrinking 'cause I didn't want to hire new people 'cause I'm very conservative, more than the male faculty. I don't want to hire someone unless I really know I can support them for a couple of years." This "motherly" behavior, sacrificing her own productivity out of concern for the well-being of others, is something she thinks her male colleagues would not consider doing. "And I know male faculty who function very differently, and they'll just like spend their money 'till it's gone," she said, "and then they'll look around and they'll go, 'Oh, what do I do [with all the people that I have promised jobs to]?'"

This professor's "mothering attitude" carries over to tasks outside the lab. "I am director of graduate studies," she stated. "[If] a student writes you an e-mail or wants to talk to you, you make an appointment. Then the student came in this morning and that was an hour and a half . . . to talk to her—but then I had to talk to her adviser." She said: "I don't get anything for that." Then she added: "Not that I need to get anything personally, I mean I actually do get personal reward. It's interesting, and I care and I want to help them out." The idea of not "getting anything" for a labor-intensive task like mentoring is a strong parallel to the unremunerated work that mothers do in raising children. Like a mother caring for her child, this professor feels that her "pay" is in the emotional reward she gets from this work and the help she provides.[72] Our survey found that female faculty spend significantly more time than their male colleagues advising, mentoring, and supervising graduate students, as well as undergraduates who are involved in research and independent studies. This work often does not benefit them in terms of promotions, prestige, or pay, and it may even hinder the acquisition of those more quantifiable rewards.

Positives of Being a Scientist Mother

In some cases, scientist mothers spoke of their dual-identity in terms of coexistence and collaboration. Although these scientists still cited negatives and struggles in trying to be both a scientist and a mother, they also see the positives that can come from holding their two identities in tension.

Spending Time Wisely

"I think [having children] has been fine, actually," said one associate professor of physics.[73] "People—young women in particular—are so worried that if you have a career in academia that there's no way that you can have kids," she continued, but she believes that outlook is false. "I would say it's easier in academia to have kids than in other careers because my time is more flexible," she explained. She has succeeded by "parenting fifty-fifty with my husband a lot and paying a lot for good child care!" Not only does she find being a scientist mother completely manageable, she thinks "that my children make me a much better scientist" because they compel her to be "extremely efficient with the use of [her] time." She asserted, "I'm not an eighty-hour-a-week worker—you can't [do that] and be with young children—but I spend every moment of my working time working very effectively." In other words, having children, she feels, is truly an asset to her career.

An associate professor of biology described how she has managed her time to balance work and family:

> Overall [it] has been fine, and the one thing I like about being a scientist is that it's flexible, and so the way I've run my career—which is part of what got me criticism from some of my colleagues, but I've pretty much ignored them—is that sometimes I take off early but I'll come back at night. Or sometimes I'm making phone calls to the school during the day, but I'm making phone calls that are related to my work at night while I'm making dinner. So I would say my main strategy has just been to make everything fairly seamless. And I have no regrets about how I've prioritized things. So, my son is just first, period. And there's no question about that, and I don't excuse that. I don't apologize for it.[74]

Although we heard from scientist mothers who prioritize their children without apology, we did not find any scientist fathers who stated so unapologetically that they put their children first.

The Mutual Benefits of Science and Mothering

Another associate professor of biology spoke about some of the positives of having children while being a scientist:

> Children are great because they . . . force you to get out and do other things instead of just focusing on work. . . . Because most of us are somewhat obsessive-compulsive. . . . [In] science there's ups and downs and things don't work, and when that happens it's always wonderful to have children, especially little children, because they're always so excited and make you feel really good about yourself, to balance out the feeling bad at work.[75]

For many scientist mothers, children keep them from spending all day and night in the lab or office, which actually helps them achieve a balance between professional and personal time. Their children provide them with a valuable perspective.

Some scientist mothers see a positive relationship between their work and home lives that benefits their children. An associate professor of biology mentioned how much her career can bring to her children's education:

> I've been interviewed on the news before about something we're doing. And so my son is very proud of that. . . . I come into the school, and I bring with me two postdocs and four microscopes, and we help the kids stain their cheek cells, you know. It's kind of a—that's meant a lot to him. So I'd say as far as being an academic parent, it kind of—it creates just a different, I think, mind-set of even—of what life, what home life is like too.[76]

It is no doubt difficult for the majority of scientist mothers to balance parenting and their careers, but many manage to do so—by adopting individual strategies, such as finding flexibility in their schedules, or collaborating with caregivers and partners to make child care manageable. These strategies are all personally negotiated rather than made institutionally available to everyone. Men, too, are using their own strategies to deal with the struggles they experience as they try to balance academic science and family life. Most male and female scientists think there are things that universities can do at the structural and cultural levels to make things better. It is to these ideas for change that we now turn.

6

A Way Forward for Universities, Science, and Scientists

On the wall of Carolyn's office, there is a bulletin board covered with pictures of babies.[1] They are the children of graduate students and postdoctoral fellows in her lab. She smiled as she said that many young researchers in her lab—both women and men—are choosing to have children because "they think they can start their family and their life." But there are not many other faculty members in her department who are as concerned as Carolyn is about young scientists, their desire to balance work and family, and their likelihood of remaining in science, she says. She also doesn't believe there are university structures in place to address the issue. She spent the early years of her career swimming upstream against a system that ignored the demands she faced at home, she recalls, and although she supports and even encourages the desire of young scientists to have children, she has come to realize that junior researchers who take time off to care for their children often find the decision negatively affects their research performance and eventually their success at finding and keeping an academic job. She struggles with how to help them realize their professional aspirations in a system that does not provide adequate support for academic scientists who want both a family and a career. Nevertheless, she tries.

How can the academic science environment be changed so that it is less daunting to strive for both a career and a family? Or should those who strive for both be left to figure out how to achieve their aspirations on their own?

To this point, we have explored the current state of academic science and the difficulties faced by those who want to be both a scientist and a parent. Here we shift our lens from analyzing the problems to looking for solutions that might move academic science forward. We hear what scientists think. For the most part, they believe that universities, science bodies like the NSF and National Institutes of Health, academic departments, and individual scientists ought to change to make it easier for scientists to sustain their careers alongside family responsibilities. We add our own voices to the mix, joining with other scholars who are exploring the changes that would make the academic science environment more responsive to and respectful of those trying to balance work and family.[2] We also explore the specific pathways through which these changes are likely to occur. Institutions, departments, and individuals all have a role to play in bringing changes to the culture and rhetoric of family life within the university environment.

Given that the top universities examined in this study are institutional leaders, the kinds of transformations they bring to their own structures might force changes to the overall structure of academic science, so that male and female scientists at all stages of their careers, in any university, no longer feel they must choose between their careers and an active family life.[3] According to legal scholar Mary Ann Mason and her colleagues, "Federal agencies and universities can make headway in solving this systemic problem . . . by setting equitable, clearly communicated baseline family responsive policies for all of their classes of researchers—not just faculty."[4] If the right changes are made, scientists will be more satisfied with their lives and careers, suffer less of a parenthood penalty, become even more committed to their jobs, and become more productive academic scientists. If such shifts are not made, the cost may be too great to bear—both for the future of academic science and for the individuals involved.

Institutional Changes

Universities and science funding agencies (like the NSF and the National Institutes of Health) are the major macrolevel institutions that shape the culture and environment of academic science. A number of policies aimed at making it easier for faculty to balance work and family have already been implemented. In September 2011, the White House and the NSF announced the "NSF Career-Life Balance Initiative."[5] This allows principal investigators to "continue grant supplements for research technicians or equivalent to sustain research when investigators need to provide family care" and to "encourage parental medical leave (paid, if possible), accommodations for dual-career couples, and part-time options." And the NSF has allocated extensive resources to funding the ADVANCE (Advancement of Women in Academic Science and Engineering Careers) studies, which have as a chief aim to promote the advancement of women in science and engineering careers.[6] Yet although many of the ADVANCE studies were completed before we finished our study, the scientists we surveyed and interviewed still argued that there is *much more to be done*.[7] In the words of one scientist: "It doesn't seem like things are changing that much."

Repeatedly, the scientists we interviewed called for structural changes—such as better support for graduate students and young scientists, affordable on-campus child care, changes to grant infrastructure that allow for family life changes, and amendments to the tenure system—that would allow them and their peers to better manage work and family. Yet they also highlighted the importance of how these policies are perceived and implemented on a day-to-day basis. Along with policy changes, then, there needs to be a change in the culture of academic science and the conversations surrounding work-life balance that academic scientists have among themselves.

Universities Need to Follow the Most Family-Friendly Corporations

S. C. Johnson is a "family company" in more ways than one: it is known for its family-friendly work policies, such as on-site day care, flexible work hours, and job sharing.[8] Research shows that the corporations that are the most family-friendly—providing flexible work schedules, sick care for children, on-site child care, and paid parental leave—have the happiest and most committed workers.[9] How different are university environments from corporate environments?

Sociologist Laurel Smith-Doerr, who compared academic scientists with scientists who work in corporations, points out that the structure of the university environment—because it operates outside the fluidity of the market—is generally more resistant to change than the structures of industry.[10] Smith-Doerr notes that most universities are more hierarchical than the private sector where science is produced. Thus, university policies may take longer to change and individual senior scientists may have much more power, but it also may be particularly difficult for women to succeed within the structure.[11] As one biologist, who is at an early point in her career as an assistant professor, explained: "[The university] is becoming more progressive . . . [but] you can see why this is a very . . . historical institution, and of course it was mostly male dominated for many years."[12] Changes to university structure are difficult to come by. Part of the challenge in getting universities to change is what one physicist called "so many layers of bureaucracy."[13] What happens, she said, is that "part A says fine, but it doesn't actually get implemented."

Structural changes to academic science are needed, however. For one thing, academic science needs to become less all-consuming of a scientist's time and devotion. A forty-six-year-old associate professor of biology, who is married to another scientist and has children aged four and seven, pointed out that the hours she is expected to work as a university professor at an elite research university are often very different from the hours expected of those working in science-related professions outside a university.[14] As she explained:

> My sister is an anesthesiologist. She works three days a week, and I think that would be nice if two days a week I could go pick up the kids after school and do something fun with them or just be with them, play with them. . . . But this isn't the job that gives you that option. . . . Sometimes I wish that I had a little more option to just cut back.

The following sections present some ways universities should change to make academic science more amenable to family life.

Change 1: Provide Child Care Centers That Are Affordable for All Scientists

The presence of an affordable child care center on their university campus was the chief thing that scientists at all ranks (even those without children) mentioned would help those with children effectively manage family and work responsibilities. Nearly one-third of the scientists surveyed said that affordable university day care is central to successfully managing both scientific work and family commitments because it helps them reduce the commute time to day care and the amount of time spent arranging for special child care situations.[15] Many of the scientists in our sample called for a child care option that is reliable, high-quality, affordable, and located on campus. It is worth noting that during the time of this study, one university where we interviewed biologists and physicists opened up a day care center in response to pressure from university faculty.

The vast majority of the universities in our sample have a university-affiliated day care program, but these services vary greatly in terms of cost, accessibility, and quality. Most important, these day care options are often not accessible to graduate students and postdoctoral fellows because of price, limited space, and long waiting lists and because these young scientists are often viewed as trainees rather than employees. A postdoctoral fellow in biology, who is married to another scientist but does not yet have children, said his current institution is providing child care benefits for the children of postdocs, but, he added, "That's pretty unusual in my experience, for postdocs to have those benefits."[16]

The cost of child care for someone on a graduate student budget is especially formidable, and scientists in our study—graduate students and tenured professors alike—note that universities need to be pressured to assist young scientists in meeting these costs. A graduate student who does not yet have children said the price of the child care his university provides is one factor that is keeping him from even considering having children, explaining that "it costs way too much for a graduate student to handle. Basically, it's the same amount as the stipend per month. . . . So, you know, I'll wait until I can earn more money for children [*laughs*]."[17]

One school that does provides assistance for junior academics is the University of Wisconsin–Madison, one of the universities in our study. For students, fees for child care are based on a sliding scale. Full-time care for a newborn is $1,620 per month, but the school provides additional assistance for graduate students through the Child Care Tuition Assistance Program (CCTAP), which typically covers 30 to 40 percent of child care expenses per semester for students.[18] Additionally, the university offers discretionary, privately funded child care grants to families facing emergencies that hinder their ability to meet the costs associated with outside child care.

Many of the schools in our sample, including the University of Texas at Austin, Rockefeller University, and Yale University, adjust child care costs according to family income. Eight of the universities in our sample offer no such consideration. It is especially important *for leader institutions* (which also tend to be those with greater financial resources, such as larger endowments) to pave the way in offering child care stipends based on income. By way of example, let's take a closer look at the day care program at Harvard University, a school that is seen by many as a symbolic and institutional leader in higher education.[19] The university has six independently run nonprofit child care centers.[20] Yet, depending on the age of the child and the location of the center, fees for full-time care range from around $3,000 per month—the most expensive center for newborns—to around $1,000 per month for the least expensive center for older preschool children. Although Harvard has some limited need-based scholarships available for faculty and staff, it seems from the information on its website that these scholarships do not extend to graduate students.[21] It appears that graduate students would be eligible only for Massachusetts state benefits as a way to defray the costs.

Hilary, the professor of biology and single mother of two teenage sons, underscored just how much of a problem the lack of high-quality affordable child care is for graduate students just beginning their careers. She raised her two children largely on her own and is one of the only faculty members in her department without a stay-at-home spouse. "They just opened child care about four years ago, for the first time," she said of her university. "That's the first time they opened child care for children under two!" Another biology professor, who is married to a biology professor and has two young sons, told us she believes difficulties surrounding access to reliable, affordable child care have a profound impact on younger scientists, an impact that is not handled well by her university.[22] "I know recently there was some kind of option for students—child care something—but then it turned out . . . their stipends are too high!" she exclaimed. "They wouldn't be eligible for [the child care assistance] . . . which is really dumb!" When universities do provide child care benefits to young scholars, it can add to the appeal of remaining in academic science. As we have seen, feeling unable to have children due to career demands, or having fewer children than desired, is a key factor that can lead scientists to consider leaving academic science.

When we move from graduate students, postdoctoral fellows, and junior faculty members to more senior faculty, we find that they have higher salaries and often more stability than the younger scientists in our study—especially when these faculty members are tenured. Still, an assistant professor of biology in his late thirties pointed out that the day care center his university recently started is much more expensive than the one where he currently sends his children.[23] As with the younger scientists, even those who do not have children often mentioned the need for more affordable, accessible day care on campus. An assistant professor in her late thirties who spent some time working in Germany told us:

> I can never understand why—after going to [Germany] where they have [a day care] right on the campus—why can't all universities have that in the buildings, and have it subsidized? . . . I don't understand that. And then you see these women running in and out. . . . And that [could be] a given that . . . for coming in as a faculty . . . you'd be able to get, you know, child care services so that you can do your work and teach. I mean, the job is hard enough. . . . [A]fter visiting Germany and seeing that, I am like, "Where the hell are we?"[24]

A married assistant professor of physics, also in her late thirties, believes the most critical action universities need to take to keep women faculty in physics is "to have good-quality [day care] and enough spots reserved for people at the university.[25] It's a no-brainer." And Jill, a married forty-year-old associate professor of physics with two children, told us:

> I gave this talk a few weeks ago, and there was a woman in the audience, a postdoc, and she is close to leaving because of the child care issue. . . . She isn't earning that much as [a] postdoc, so she's like, "I'm going to leave, I'm going to get a high-paid job. I can buy my kids better stuff. I can afford child care."
>
> . . . So if you are a woman in science and you're the major breadwinner for your family . . . then you just, you just can't have kids [or] you have to leave the field. [26]

At the most elite research universities in the country, even those in tenure-track science positions often cannot afford or do not have access to university-sponsored day care. University administrators ought to be struck by this fact—and, as we have seen, if they want to keep the best and brightest young scientists from leaving their institutions because of family concerns, they have to do something to change it. It should be noted that the day care center at Rice University (where Elaine currently teaches) has been a major factor in supporting her work as well as that of her scientist husband. Rice University, by giving faculty who take a parental leave one full semester off with full pay, is notably progressive compared with many other schools; nevertheless, it does not offer subsidies for graduate students, although that is one of the recommendations of its recent NSF-funded ADVANCE study.

Change 2: Provide Better Nonstandard Child Care Benefits

At the time we were writing this book, an American University assistant professor took her infant, who woke up with a fever, to a class she had to teach, and at one point she breast-fed her to quiet her down, raising a media firestorm.[27] "The single mother worried that she had no good child-care options," an article in the *Washington Post* explained.

Typical day-to-day child care will often not meet the needs of academics, many of whom work beyond the nine-to-five workday and have job responsibilities that cannot be rescheduled or delayed. A recent report from the American Council on Education echoes the sentiment of many scientists in our study in stating that "childcare available during regular work hours (i.e., Monday through Friday, 6 a.m. to 6 p.m.) would still be insufficient to address the needs of most full-time tenured and tenure-track faculty with children."[28] This is especially the case with academic scientists. Not only do they often work very long hours—a lab experiment can require all-night observation, for example—but they also have to travel for conferences, and many of them are partners with someone in the same career, who also has nonstandard work hours. Thus, they are in particular need of nonstandard child care benefits.

James, the physicist we met earlier who decided to postpone marriage until he and his wife completed postdoctoral fellowships in two different places, puts nonstandard child care at the top of his list of how universities can assist academic scientists who are balancing careers and family. He feels it should not be up to individual faculty members to come up with solutions on their own and believes that providing emergency child care for faculty and all science researchers "when the school is closed, when the kid is sick, when something unexpected happens" is the single measure that would make scientists who have children "not look so different from our peers [who do not have children]" when it comes to research productivity. He continued:

> The single biggest problem that we encounter is emergency child care or nonstandard child care or what you do when . . . *you get the call* [his emphasis]. That's what we call it. You know, your daughter is sick, you have to come pick her up, and I say, "No, I have to write this. I have to submit the proposal. If I don't push the button . . . you know, I'm out hundreds of thousands of dollars." So universities have the capability to have sick child care. Yes, you can drop them off; they'll have, you know, appropriate staff. . . . So we keep saying over and over and over again, what do you—what's needed? And it's emergency child care. . . . [I]f life gets harder instead of easier in that regard, it's going to be very discouraging. And I talked about how people might think situations are equal, but they are not. I'm sure that statistically when, you know, the call comes or somebody has to go pick up the kid, I am willing to bet that this is a serious detriment on female careers—that they miss that planning meeting on the proposal or they are not there at that critical moment.

In fact, the institution where James works does provide backup child care to mildly ill children, which makes us wonder whether the program is not easy to access, not applicable to his situation, or not well advertised, or if there are forces at the departmental level that discourage him from taking advantage of such resources. It is important and exciting that some nonstandard child care options are available in the university environment, but for them to be effective, scientists must be aware of their existence *and* feel comfortable taking advantage of them.

Other scientists raised the idea of nonstandard flex accounts for child care—a fund they can use in any way, whether for after-hours day care or to hire a nanny who can travel. One thirty-eight-year-old assistant professor of physics told us that she had to pay out of pocket for a nanny to travel with her to conferences, so she "fought for financial aid to help to take a nanny along to conferences." She admitted that she did this primarily to benefit the younger women who would come after her in science, with support and encouragement from her husband, who is also a physicist. In his words, "The women that are coming after you, if there is a program in place that will pay for a caregiver to make travel possible, you know, it would be very helpful."

Another form of nontraditional child care would be for universities to provide relief from grant management responsibilities when the birth of a child makes it impossible to continue as the principal investigator of a grant. Although many universities provide parental leave and stop the tenure clock when a faculty member has a child, principal investigators must still run their research and grants. For many scientists, managing funded research can be even more difficult to navigate than their other university responsibilities after the birth of a child. A male associate professor of physics shared that his

> wife got a PhD in physics and quit because the work hours would be long all the way through her child-rearing years. The American system gives women almost no accommodation for having children and very little choice here. Tenure-clock extensions or teaching relief do *not* address the problem, which is that an interruption in funding caused by family issues can lead to a downward spiral in research productivity and support. Federal grant agencies have to respond with policies to specifically address the issue.[29]

There is some hope on the horizon, however. Funding agencies are beginning to allow grants to be paused or extended upon the birth of a child or when there is some other family-related challenge to data collection.

Elaine has some personal experience in this regard. Her first child was born soon after Elaine began the research for this book. At the time, she was in the midst of beginning data collection as part of the NSF grant that supported this research. During the three months that she had a full semester of paid parental leave, the piece of the data collection she was responsible for slowed dramatically. Although her absence was difficult for colleagues and students, the data collection was still finished in the time allotted by the grant thanks to Anne's work and the help of an able project manager—certainly not a widely available option due to decreases in university-funded support staff. The birth of a child could be a more costly challenge for natural scientists running grant-funded research, who often do much more time-sensitive research than social scientists. What would help is research grant funding that could be allocated to child care.[30] From a physics graduate student in her late twenties we heard:

> Because the way the grant rules are, you can't use an NSF grant to pay someone to take care of your kid while you're at an observing trip. . . . I mean, a lot of the two-astronomer couples with kids who are managing, the only way they manage is that they have free child care from one set of parents. And so it's, "OK, we're going to a conference. Here are the kids." But that's not a sustainable model for how to get women and keep women in the field. And I mean, 'cause it is a professional expense, but you can't use the grant money for it.[31]

Change 3: Make Leaves and Stopping Tenure Clocks Automatic

Of the thirty-one universities included in our sample, twenty of them—roughly two-thirds—offer some sort of family leave beyond the twelve weeks of unpaid leave required by the Family and Medical Leave Act. These extended leave policies vary significantly by university and often apply only to tenure-track faculty. For example, the University of Minnesota gives female faculty six weeks of paid leave upon the birth of a child, biological fathers two weeks of paid leave and four weeks of unpaid leave, and adoptive parents two weeks of paid leave and four weeks of unpaid leave. Harvard University offers up to four weeks of paid leave for new parents who are primary caregivers and up to thirteen weeks of unpaid leave for birth, adoptive, or foster mothers. Yale University offers new parents up to one semester of unpaid leave, while the California Institute of Technology provides additional leave only to employees who are medically disabled due to their pregnancy or childbirth.

Policies regarding leave are sometimes different for graduate students and postdoctoral fellows. The University of Minnesota offers paid and unpaid leave to graduate students who serve as teaching assistants but not to other graduate students. Harvard offers graduate students a period of accommodation through an adjustment of the number of years in graduate school, but no leave time; Harvard does, however, offer postdoctoral fellows the same leave as faculty. In many situations, if a person decides to take a longer leave, there may be a loss of pay, insurance, or child care eligibility.

We suggest that research universities should offer an automatic one-semester paid leave upon the birth of a child for all ranks of scientists, from graduate students through full professors. The new parent should have to apply to *forgo* the leave rather than need to apply to *take* the leave. Scientists who become parents would then not have to informally negotiate whether or not to take a parental leave, or wonder how taking a leave will impact how more senior scientists in their departments view them. Making leave automatic may help men who want to be involved parents sidestep male-mystique and ideal-worker norms.

Along with paid leaves upon the birth or adoption of a child ought to come a mandatory halt of the tenure clock. As Evan described in chapter 4, when it came to child care, he often found himself saying, "Sorry, can't do it. I got to work on this, I need to get tenure." The demands of getting tenure made him feel it was acceptable and necessary to put work before his family.

For young academic scientists to start families and to have a robust family life alongside their careers, universities will need to change tenure expectations and requirements. One young biologist in her early thirties who has completed a postdoctoral fellowship suggests the biggest problem is the race to publish, which requires her to work her "butt off every single second."[32] As she sees it now, "It's like impossible—you can't go on maternity leave and be on a tenure-track position. . . . Being on a tenure-track position, you have no time for anything else."

One of the changes that the scientists we talked with wanted to see was the possibility of time off and reentry for tenure-track positions. An assistant professor of physics in her late thirties, who is married to another physicist, explained that part of the reason she does not have children is directly tied to tenure. She revealed:

> I was thirty-six when I was hired for the junior faculty position, and I have been here for three years, . . . and tenure is either five years or maybe starting at six and, you know, you kind of start worrying about the timing . . . the age factor, it sort of makes everything seem more difficult and complicated so, so I think that's the struggle right now.

Many women spoke of similar concerns. In response, universities might allow scientists who are in their childbearing years to take a couple of years off the tenure clock to have or care for young children.

The scientists we spoke with also thought it would be helpful if universities developed options for part-time positions for tenure-track faculty members that could be used for a specified period (up to five years) as personal needs arise. In addition, universities should guard against penalties for résumé gaps that result from dependent care, such as time taken off to have a child, especially given that the tenure track is stretching much longer and overlapping with the childbearing years more than ever before.[33]

An associate professor of physics whose wife stays at home with their children told us that his university now "has this program where if you have a child when you're coming up for tenure, they automatically grant you, I think, an extension."[34] An associate professor of biology in her early forties who recently received tenure told us that while her university has a policy that allows faculty to stop the tenure clock when they have a baby, she was not eligible for this benefit because she had her children when she was a postdoctoral fellow.[35] She also said her biggest needs came later, however, when her children were a little older, but she was not able to stop the tenure clock then. Current policies, therefore, should be altered to make tenure clock stops more flexible so they can fit the needs of individual scientists.

Cultural Shifts

Even when helpful policies are in place, some scientists feel they cannot actually take advantage of the benefits because of the stigma associated with taking time off from research and university life. A twenty-nine-year-old postdoctoral fellow in physics who is married to another physicist explained it this way: "I've heard conflicting advice about being able to stop your tenure clock. I have heard that even though that's a great thing, women don't actually do it because even though the tenure clock is supposed to be stopped for a year while they're having a child, it's held against them."[36] A cultural shift must accompany and complement a policy shift if academic science is to become more family-friendly.

Academic science must show itself to be more accepting of a commitment to parenting and must help foster this commitment. Norms have to change. It is not enough for policies to be in place on paper if real people on the ground do not accept them.

A cultural shift is most needed when it comes to implementing policy changes. An assistant professor of physics, who is married to another physicist and has two young boys, laughs in spite of herself as she recalled how hard it was to actually receive the benefits her university's policies were meant to provide:

> These policies are all very good, but in the end, the expectation is that I, you know, publish and travel during the time that I have a very small child under one year old, just like everybody else. . . . My boss—basically the director—will say, "Oh, yes, you're giving birth next week, and . . . you know, just don't do anything, we'll do everything. But can you write this grant and we'll submit it in a month?" . . . He's saying: you're expected to be here with a three-month-old baby. . . . I think the policies are there, but the real—the personal sensitivity—of especially men—to the issue of being torn between your work and caring for a young infant [is not there].[37]

A twenty-nine-year-old biology graduate student, who has a sixteen-month-old son, expressed a similar concern.[38] She explained that although there are various resources in place for new parents that allow them to take time off from work, they feel that if they utilize this time off, they will fall behind their colleagues. Within the current culture of academic science, the sense seems to be that any time off—even that which is legitimized by university policy—is seen as a detriment and a compromise to scientific progress. Ultimately, policies are not implemented in a vacuum; they are shaped by institutional culture. Therefore, policy changes must be complemented by a culture in which they can be meaningfully enacted.

Department Cultures

Academic departments are the local organizations that mediate how policies developed at the university level are implemented for individual scientists. They often control, for example, the application of family leave policies and whether it is deemed acceptable for a scientist to devote time to family. Scientists cited specific changes that departments should make to be more amenable to family life. We argue that one of the most important things to change is how departments help scientist parents cope with department-level responsibilities, such as serving on hiring and policy committees. An associate professor of physics in his early fifties, who has two preteen children and is married to another physicist, said that departments can help "with committee assignments or flexibility or just saying, 'You need to go [to get your child]? Sure we will reschedule it' . . . instead of, 'No, we are going to make this decision or make these assignments today.'"[39]

Changes to departmental culture often require conscious, sustained effort and key leaders. A senior physicist in his early sixties recalled with pride the major changes he led in his department over the course of his career.[40] "I was first chair in '95, and we only had one woman faculty member on our faculty at that point," he recalled. "But we were starting to have more women in our physics major." In response, the department recognized that it need[ed] to expand our graduate program to accept more women" despite the fact that "they really weren't qualified initially . . . if we were looking strictly at performance on the Graduate Record Exam, for example." The department decided that, "If [we] needed additional . . . undergraduate training, then that was OK," he said, "because we needed to break out of the mold." In other words, he used his power as department chair to foster gender equity in the graduate program—and he was willing to bend rules, maneuver structures, and challenge established norms to do so. He also utilized outside institutional supports. "We had a panel come in from . . . [a] women's group through the American Physical Society, that came and reviewed our department, looked at our policies, suggested various things like having luncheons for women, and we managed to get [a corporation] to fund that," he said. Unlike larger university structures, departments allow for this sort of malleability and immediate action. With this in mind, we offer some suggestions for how departments might make it easier for scientists to negotiate family life.

Change 1: Develop Checks and Balances at the Department Level

As we have just seen, the chair of a department is often a kind of organizational gatekeeper, determining how a department puts policies into place and the kind of culture that is created and maintained within that department. Scientists think that chairs have so much power in implementing family-related policies that they often mentioned that universities could do a better job of making sure that there are checks and balances in place to ensure that this power is used to promote, rather than discourage, work-family balance. And many universities are beginning to adopt different hiring practices to rectify the gender imbalance in science.[41] A biologist in her early forties said that, in general, her department is helpful, and it does not matter whether the department chair is a man or a woman, but she also said more checks and balances are "needed to ensure that things are more egalitarian."[42] She is particularly concerned about the power that department chairs have to make independent and influential hiring decisions. She would like to see this power regulated by a formal rule that protects scientists who may experience family constraints.

When a department chair is sympathetic to the family demands of a scientist parent, it can make things much easier. One associate professor of physics with two young boys said she had "relief from teaching the semester after each of them [was born] and that was a no-brainer; I just had to ask my chair and she said of course."[43] But a physicist in his late thirties, who works as a postdoctoral fellow and whose wife stays at home with their children, said that the wrong department chair can make things disastrous for young women in science—particularly in a discipline like physics, where women are especially underrepresented.[44] He remembered "a nontenured female faculty member [who] had a kid and it was just, like, the end of the world, you know. The department chairman pretty much made it clear that that was not acceptable, and so she ended up going to another institution." According to this postdoctoral fellow, the faculty member lost her job at the whim of a department chair who was not supportive of family life for his colleagues.

In other cases, department chairs may not explicitly adopt an oppositional attitude toward family but may simply be unaware of the pressures of family life. (This can be the case for both male and female chairs, whether or not they have children themselves.) When the chair has partial power to establish the permanency of each faculty member, postdoctoral fellow, or graduate student in the department, this lack of understanding can have serious consequences. An assistant professor of biology whose wife currently stays home to care for their sons, aged four and seven, said his chair couldn't understand his need for a reliable career to support his family:

> So my chairman . . . is a very successful researcher. . . . He didn't have any kids. And so I just felt like talking with him and trying to explain to him the urgency of this stuff was just lost on him. . . . I needed to make money. . . . I need to know where I'm going to be in a year. I need to know is there a position here.[45]

The chair replied with an ambiguous but culturally acceptable response: "Well, you know, we'll see"—ostensibly meaning, he'll see whether the biologist receives grants or tenure. In order to protect his family, the biologist had to go against the norm of waiting on a tenure committee and explain with great urgency, "I gotta know . . . I got a wife and kids, and . . . I can't be saying, 'Well, we'll see what happens in a year.'" Once the chair understood the predicament and "kind of got the picture," the biologist said, he utilized his clout to write a contract guaranteeing a job the next year. In hindsight, this biologist feels that he "was very pushy," yet it was only through this effort that he was able to provide the stability his family requires. Ultimately, he was able to meet his needs through the department chair, but other scientists might not feel as empowered to confront a critical gatekeeper in this way.

The scheduling of many day-to-day activities is often determined at the department level. Scientists point out that departments are often insensitive to how an issue as basic as scheduling can impact their family lives. For example, department seminars with outside speakers often begin after 4:00 p.m., making it difficult for faculty members to attend if they need to pick up their children from day care or school. A biologist mentioned that her department often schedules meetings early in the morning—before 8:00 a.m.—making it impossible for her to get to the meeting on time unless her husband can take time off work to take their children to school.[46] She believes that the timing of the meetings communicates implicit assumptions about the kinds of family arrangements that scientists have. If departments were more conscious of scheduling in a family-friendly way, it would go further toward keeping women in science than, for example, counting the number of women interviewed for a given faculty position.

One of our respondents called the university a feudal system, in which full professors and the principal investigators of the major grants can be thought of as the lords of the property, in control of all those who work below them.[47] Clearly, this gives them a large amount of power. The graduate students and postdoctoral fellows we interviewed—in both physics and biology departments—explained that it can be extremely difficult to work under an adviser who doesn't appreciate the difficulties of balancing work and family. A young graduate student in physics explained:

> It's just kind of the nature of who you work for . . . I think—well I think my adviser is a little bit on the more workaholic side. . . . I mean, it's a real challenge, especially for, you know, if you're a woman and you have children, you know? You want to—you have got to dedicate such a large part of your life, all of your life. . . . It's hard to split that up between raising kids as well.[48]

A twenty-eight-year-old female graduate student in physics, who is single, said that at her university, they have

> tried to get parental leave into the grad student contracts and they just won't do it 'cause they keep saying, "Well, we don't want to formalize the relationship," and that way it's between you and your adviser. It's like, well, that's great if you've got a nice adviser with lots of money, but if you don't, or if your adviser is short on money, like, that just doesn't work.[49]

Change 2: Empower Individuals to Change Cultures

Individual senior scientists—those who have influence in the university and have flourished in the field—can help transform the academic science environment so that it better responds to the difficulties of being both a scientist and a parent. These scientists are key actors in initiating and implementing change on the ground level. They have to force institutions to change in order to enable and facilitate cultural shifts.

The scientists we interviewed recognized that one way to bring change to their institution was to begin telling different stories about how they understood their place within the institution, whether or not others agreed with these stories. Cognitive scientists recognize the specific power of *stories* in the development of cognitive schema (interpretive frameworks, such as a scientific understanding); when concepts and ways of thinking are bundled within stories, they are easier to believe, apprehend, and remember.[50]

One way scientists can change the conversation surrounding the balance of work and children is to change the struggle from a "woman's issue" to a "family issue." In this way, it becomes a story that both male and female scientists should tell. This is an important change because issues that are viewed as particular to women are often seen as private matters and different from what might be important to science as a whole. Gayle, a professor of physics we introduced earlier, said:

> I've seen this time and time and time again. Guys get dispensation to leave because they have problems all the time and nobody talks about it. So, that's one of the things that's kind of unfair—the other thing that's unfair is that women are fighting for these rights and we get some of them, right? We are getting a little more maternity leave; we are getting a little more, allowing people to roll the tenure clock back. So it's getting better, and people are trying to be more supportive of women, definitely that's better. But we also have the backlash of other people saying "Oh, of course she is going to get that, she is a woman."[51]

Many women were very vocal about the ways that being a scientist affected their family lives, but they were also adamant that *men* need to be involved in discussions about family responsibilities and roles. As a result, they created new spaces for new ways of understanding gender roles. This was particularly important among the physicists we talked with; because there is a much lower proportion of women in physics than in biology, physicists were much more likely to think of the conversation surrounding family life as a woman's conversation.

Women also told stories about expanding the jurisdiction of their core roles. Sociologist Andrew Abbott introduced ideas about professional jurisdiction.[52] In the legal sphere, for example, as the number of divorces increased in the last century, divorce lawyers had to determine whether managing clients' emotional and psychological issues fell within their professional jurisdiction. Most divorce lawyers decided it did not, sometimes forming partnerships or referral networks with psychologists, counselors, or other professionals who could provide such services.[53] In medicine, physicians and nurses have long negotiated their professional expertise vis-à-vis each other.[54] More recently, nurses and other medical professionals have considered whether aspects of complementary and alternative medicine fall within or are relevant to their professional jurisdiction.[55]

One female scientist who has two young children talked about how she took over unused space within her department to create a breastfeeding room for young mothers.[56] And because having children limited her ability to travel, she developed her research locally, within the laboratories of her own university, providing more opportunities to mentor students and expand her on-campus role. She said that while other members of her department might collaborate with international colleagues in person, she is happy to do so remotely and to continue her research on her own university campus, where she is able to direct students and carve out a space that works for her.

Scientists who want academic science to be more family-friendly continually seek out allies for assistance and encouragement. Female physicists, in particular, seek out other women (and men) for support. For example, Jill described the time when she and three other women in her department were all pregnant as a life-changing moment. The support they provided one another helped her overcome self-doubt and embrace her new role as a mother alongside her ongoing role as a physicist. She recalled:

> That was fantastic. That really helped my sanity because seeing that my experiences of frustration, trying to balance things and not getting enough work in, resentment toward male colleagues who could just do everything because they could somehow, that was a common theme amongst us, and it wasn't me being crazy, do you know what I mean?

In addition, a few female physicists spoke of the role their husbands played as allies in their success. One respondent, whose husband is also a physicist, said that he not only made sacrifices to his career to ensure her success but also took on additional responsibilities as a father and even helped her with her research. She said that at home they discussed each other's research problems, and he helped her work through research quagmires. Female physicists have also relied on networks—composed of other women and, most commonly, supportive men—that validate their identities as women and mothers in science.

From Carolyn, the successful senior biologist, we hear just how important individuals can be in supporting those around them and leading the way for those who come after them—as well as how valuable family can prove to be in the life of a scientist. Carolyn's father was one of her most important allies. She leaves us with these words:

> I can point to what individuals did for me as a person to better myself . . . and what are the kind of seeds that I was given that helped that part of me grow. . . . And that is kind of what got me through this whole early part of my career. And I would say now, what matters more . . . [is] I want to be that person that helps the next group. . . . [T]he best advice I have ever had is from my dad . . . my dad was in the military. . . . I was coming up for tenure. I was under a lot of stress. I told him, "I can't figure out these people, I don't know." And he was like, "You don't know what stress is." And he said, "Stress is being behind enemy lines in a helicopter, it's pouring down rain, they're shooting at you, and you have to jump out. So you know they are going to try and kill you." And he said, "And it's your first jump. That's stressful." And I said, "Oh my God! How did you do it?" and he said, "You put yourself out of your own mind and you say: I am here, I am ready to go, I am here, I must be qualified because the people who were my commanders said you will do this, we've trained you, you are ready to go. So I put my confidence in them and then I realized I had these terrified eighteen-year-olds looking at me and I have to set the example, and so when I jump, it is for them." So he said, "I would get to the door because I had the faith in the people that put me there, and I jumped because I have to set an example for the people that would follow in my footsteps." And that is the best advice I have ever gotten, and I feel like now I am jumping for the people coming behind me. For me, being able to articulate that, it is a very nice feeling to know that it is not about me at all anymore, it is about the next stage.

Appendix A

THE STUDY

The data for this book come from the Perceptions of Women in Academic Science (PWAS) project, a study of the ways scientists at elite research universities understand the social dynamics that influence the perceptions, contributions, and career prospects of women and men in science, with emphasis on the distinctive expectations and constraints experienced by female scientists. The project incorporates both quantitative and qualitative data, utilizing a survey (called "Influences on Science Career") of scientists at top American universities and in-depth interviews with a subsample of survey respondents.

Project participants were randomly selected from among academic scientists at the top twenty U.S. graduate programs in biology and physics as determined by the National Research Council (NRC) report *Research-Doctorate Programs in the United States* (1995),[1] considered by many to be the gold standard of graduate program rankings. Biologists were drawn from all four of the subdisciplines recognized by the NRC: biochemistry and molecular biology; ecology, evolution, and behavior; molecular and general genetics; and cell and developmental biology. Because many universities have separate academic departments devoted to these specialties, the rankings of which may differ, the number of universities that have top biology programs is more than twenty. In addition, because the proportion of women in physics is so low, we included astronomy and astrophysics departments as well, increasing the proportion of women in the sampling frame and also accommodating joint departments that house, for example, physics and astronomy together.

Due to the age of the NRC rankings, we cross-referenced them with the 2008 *U.S. News & World Report* "Best Graduate Programs" rankings. Though these rankings were conducted more than a decade apart and employing somewhat different criteria, the two ranking systems proved mostly consistent. The following universities are included in our study:

Baylor College of Medicine
California Institute of Technology
Columbia University
Cornell University
Duke University
Harvard University
Johns Hopkins University
Massachusetts Institute of Technology
Princeton University
Rockefeller University
Scripps Research Institute
Stanford University
University of California, Berkeley
University of California, Davis
University of California, Los Angeles
University of California, San Diego
University of California, San Francisco
University of California, Santa Barbara
University of Chicago
University of Colorado Boulder
University of Georgia
University of Illinois
University of Maryland
University of Michigan
University of Pennsylvania
University of Texas at Austin
University of Washington
University of Wisconsin–Madison
Washington University
Yale University

We examined biology and physics in particular because they are core science disciplines with very different levels of female representation. While the number of women in biology is on the increase at all points on the faculty career track, the number of women in physics remains quite low. We studied the top twenty U.S. graduate programs because these programs generate most of the leaders in the field. Research finds that those who attend elite graduate programs disproportionately become leaders in all fields, including the sciences, where scholars find that these "thought leaders" exercise significant influence on science policy. Thus, understanding the experiences with work and family life of faculty members at these elite institutions is important for anyone considering the influence of work-family balance on scientists' job satisfaction and even their attrition from science.

The universe of biologists and physicists at elite universities—consisting of more than 14,000 individuals from 100 departments at thirty-one universities—was compiled from department web pages, university directories, and calls to departments. An initial sample of 3,500 scientists was chosen randomly from and divided equally among all graduate students, postdoctoral fellows, assistant professors, associate professors, and full professors in departments with the top twenty biology, physics, and astronomy/astrophysics graduate programs. Excluding 45 individuals who were misidentified and did not meet our criteria for inclusion in terms of rank or department left 3,455 potential survey respondents.

Surveys were administered online and by phone from November 2008 through February 2009. Each potential respondent was mailed a personalized contact letter that included fifteen dollars that the scientist could keep even if he or she did not participate. Next, respondents were e-mailed eight to ten times by the survey firm. The firm, Shulman, Ronca, and Buchavales, Inc. (SRBI), sent each potential respondent a unique ID with which to log into a website and complete the survey. After the reminder e-mails, SRBI phoned nonresponders up to twenty times. Only 7.5 percent of the respondents completed the survey over the telephone; 92 percent completed the Web-based survey. The overall response rate of 72 percent (2,503 respondents) is exceptional for a survey of academics. By comparison, Preston's study of retention and exit from science careers by one university's graduates received a 35 percent response rate,[2] and Van Anders's study of graduate students at the University of Western Ontario generated only an 18 percent completion rate.[3] Even the highly successful Carnegie Commission study of faculty generated just a 60 percent response rate.[4] The final PWAS survey sample included 684 graduate students, 504 postdoctoral fellows, 447 assistant professors, 325 associate professors, and 543 full professors for a total of

1,300 biologists and 1,203 physicists from 100 academic departments at thirty-one universities.

The survey asked scientists how they became interested in science, how they experienced science as an undergraduate, and how they balanced family and work responsibilities; it also asked them about the positives and negatives of working at their particular university and other questions related to influences on and satisfaction with a science career. The survey requested information about academic rank, publications, grant funding, and demographic characteristics. Semistructured interviews explored these and other subjects in greater detail, including efforts at public outreach through media interviews, discussions in public forums, and volunteering in children's science classrooms.

From a disproportionate stratified random sample of survey respondents that oversampled women, 216 scientists were selected for in-depth interviews. Between 2009 and 2011, a total of 150 interviews (a 69 percent response rate) were completed with 84 biologists and 66 physicists. Each respondent was interviewed once, either face-to-face or by phone, for between twenty minutes and two hours. The interviews were independently transcribed, edited, and systematically coded for themes related to the central research questions, achieving an intercoder reliability of .90, calculated as a simple percentage. Semistructured interviews capture the narrative aspect of the research, which build upon the quantitative analyses. The narratives scientists communicate are important because narratives are discursive practices individuals use to produce social and psychological realities in conversation with the interviewer,[5] and because both memory and perception, whether accurate or not, strongly influence current belief and action.[6] Moreover, personal identities are constructed through language,[7] such that if male and female scientists use different languages to describe science disciplines, they likely view their scientific identities in different ways. Only through qualitative analysis of discursive material can such dynamics be investigated.

Appendix B

WEB SURVEY

SURVEY INVITATION LETTER

Thank you for participating in this fifteen-minute survey sponsored by Rice University, Southern Methodist University and funded by the National Science Foundation. We emphasize that this is a research study and all information you provide is protected by law and will be kept strictly confidential. Your identity will not be disclosed in any findings that are disseminated about the study.

To increase our understanding of the factors that influenced your decision to enter science and help you maintain a science career it is vitally important that we gather systematic information on this topic. Please be assured that all individual-level and department-level data will be kept completely confidential and secured. Analyses will be based on aggregates and findings reported such that neither individuals nor their departments can be identified in the results. Our security and confidentiality protocols have been reviewed and approved by both Rice University's and Southern Methodist University's Committees on Human Subjects. In addition, members of our senior faculty advisory board have also received this data collection protocol.

If you have questions, or want to confirm the legitimacy of this research, SRBI National Public Policy Research Center can be reached toll-free at 1-800-772-9287. Please ask for study #4588. For concerns about your rights as a research participant, please contact Nancy Nisbett at Rice University (nnisbett@rice.edu) and ask for study #09-008E. For any other questions about the study, please email Elaine Howard Ecklund directly at ehe@rice.edu.

Thanks again for your participation.

Sincerely,

Elaine Howard Ecklund

Anne E. Lincoln

WEB AND PHONE SURVEY

First some questions about your academic career.

1. Which one of the following best describes your title or rank?
   1. Graduate student
   2. Postdoctoral fellow
   3. Assistant professor
   4. Associate professor, with tenure
   5. Professor, with tenure
2. Which one of the following comes closest to your main discipline?
   1. Biology
   2. Physics
   3. Or something else (please specify: ________________)

[IF Q1 = 1]

3a. In what year will you receive your PhD?: ________________
[RANGE: 2008–50]

[IF Q1 = 2, 3, 4, or 5]

3b. In what year did you receive your PhD?: ________________
[RANGE: 1900–2008]

Scholarly Productivity

4. In your entire academic career, about how many peer-reviewed articles have you published in academic or professional journals?
5. In your entire academic career, about how much research grant funding have you received in terms of overall dollar amount (including overhead)?
6. For how many of your funded grants have you been the principal investigator?
7. Have you ever received an award that recognizes your research?
   1. Yes (go to Q9)
   2. No
8. Could you name the most prestigious award (besides grant funding) that you have received for your research accomplishments?
9. Thinking across the last academic year (2007–8), about how many hours per week on average did you spend in activities related to your career as a scientist?

[IF Q1 = 3, 4, or 5]

10. Thinking across the last academic year (2007–8), about how many hours per week on average did you spend advising, mentoring, or supervising the following?
    a. Official undergraduate advisees
        1. Less than an hour a week
        2. One to two hours a week
        3. Three to five hours per week
        4. Six to ten hours per week
        5. More than 10 hours per week
        6. Did not advise, mentor, or supervise
    b. Informal undergraduate advisees
        1. Less than an hour a week
        2. One to two hours a week
        3. Three to five hours per week
        4. Six to ten hours per week
        5. More than 10 hours per week
        6. Did not advise, mentor, or supervise
    c. Undergraduate research assistants; undergraduate honors students; undergraduates in independent study with you
        1. Less than an hour a week
        2. One to two hours a week
        3. Three to five hours per week
        4. Six to ten hours per week
        5. More than 10 hours per week
        6. Did not advise, mentor, or supervise
    d. Graduate or professional students
        1. Less than an hour a week
        2. One to two hours a week
        3. Three to five hours per week
        4. Six to ten hours per week
        5. More than 10 hours per week
        6. Did not advise, mentor, or supervise
    e. Postdoctoral associates; postdoctoral fellows; research associates, technicians
        1. Less than an hour a week
        2. One to two hours a week
        3. Three to five hours per week

4. Six to ten hours per week
5. More than 10 hours per week
6. Did not advise, mentor, or supervise

f. Junior faculty
1. Less than an hour a week
2. One to two hours a week
3. Three to five hours per week
4. Six to ten hours per week
5. More than 10 hours per week
6. Did not advise, mentor, or supervise

11. Compared to peers in your subfield and at your rank nationwide, how would you rate your overall level of research productivity on a 10 point scale, where 1 is much less productive and 10 is much more productive?

1 2 3 4 5 6 7 8 9 10

[IF Q1 = 3, 4, or 5]

12. Now I'd like you to tell me the number of committees and professional associations you served on in the last academic year (2007–8).

Total: ________________

b. How many have you chaired?
c. How many have been graduate student thesis committees?
d. Administrative committees in your department, unit, or college?
e. University-wide committees, initiatives, task forces, etc.
f. External committees (e.g., advisory committees, review committees)
g. Positions as an officer or board member of a disciplinary association
h. Positions on an editorial board
i. Have you served on any other committees or professional associations?

Yes (which ones?):
No

[IF Q1 = 3, 4, or 5]

13. Have you served in any of the following administrative capacities at your current university?

a. Department chair
   1. Served in last academic year (2007–8)
   2. Currently serving
   3. Have ever served
   4. Have never served
b. Director of a center or laboratory (including your own laboratory)
   1. Served in last academic year (2007–8)
   2. Currently serving
   3. Have ever served
   4. Have never served
c. Extension leader
   1. Served in last academic year (2007–8)
   2. Currently serving
   3. Have ever served
   4. Have never served
d. Dean, Associate Dean or Assistant Dean
   1. Served in last academic year (2007–8)
   2. Currently serving
   3. Have ever served
   4. Have never served
e. Director of Undergraduate Study
   1. Served in last academic year (2007–8)
   2. Currently serving
   3. Have ever served
   4. Have never served
f. Director of Graduate Study
   1. Served in last academic year (2007–8)
   2. Currently serving
   3. Have ever served
   4. Have never served
g. Have you served in any other administrative capacities at your current university?

Yes (which ones?):

No

14. Please tell me how frequently the following statements apply to life at your university

a. I experience joy in my work.
  1. Never
  2. Rarely
  3. Sometimes
  4. Often
  5. Very often
b. I spend weekends and vacations working.
  1. Never
  2. Rarely
  3. Sometimes
  4. Often
  5. Very often
c. I think about work even when I am doing something else.
  1. Never
  2. Rarely
  3. Sometimes
  4. Often
  5. Very often
d. I feel respected by the students I teach or advise.
  1. Never
  2. Rarely
  3. Sometimes
  4. Often
  5. Very often
  6. I do not teach or advise students
e. I feel respected by others in my peer group (other graduate students, postdoctoral fellows, faculty).
  1. Never
  2. Rarely
  3. Sometimes
  4. Often
  5. Very often
f. I feel respected by the clerical and administrative staff.
  1. Never
  2. Rarely
  3. Sometimes
  4. Often

5. Very often

[IF Q1 = 3, 4, or 5]

15. Overall, how satisfied are you being a faculty member at your current institution?
    1. Very dissatisfied
    2. Somewhat dissatisfied
    3. Neither dissatisfied nor satisfied
    4. Somewhat satisfied
    5. Very satisfied

[IF Q1 = 1]

16. Overall, how satisfied are you being a graduate student at your current institution?
    1. Very dissatisfied
    2. Somewhat dissatisfied
    3. Neither dissatisfied nor satisfied
    4. Somewhat satisfied
    5. Very satisfied

[IF Q1 = 2]

17. Overall, how satisfied are you with being a postdoctoral fellow at your current institution?
    1. Very dissatisfied
    2. Somewhat dissatisfied
    3. Neither dissatisfied nor satisfied
    4. Somewhat satisfied
    5. Very satisfied
18. From among the following, please describe the most significant reason in your choice to pursue a career in science. (select ONE response)
    1. I had a significant mentor at the grade school level.
    2. I had a significant mentor at the high school level.
    3. I had a significant mentor at the college level.
    4. I had a special aptitude for science that was discovered in my grade school years.
    5. I had a special aptitude for science that was discovered in my high school years.
    6. I had a special aptitude for science that was discovered in my college years.

7. My parents or a family member encouraged me to pursue a science career.
8. It was suggested by a career counselor or career personality test.
9. The job opportunities or salary.
10. I just always had a natural intellectual curiosity for science.
11. Awards/scholarships were a significant influence.
12. I decided largely to pursue science on my own without much influence from other sources.
13. Or is there some other most important factor? (please specify: ________________)

19. As an undergraduate, which of the following most closely describes the major that you chose when you first entered college?
    1. Physical science (i.e., physics, chemistry)
    2. Life science (i.e., biology)
    3. Social science (i.e., sociology, psychology)
    4. Humanities (i.e., English, history)
    5. Professional program (i.e., business)
    6. Engineering
    7. Mathematics
    8. Computer science
20. Which of the following **most closely** describes the major with which you graduated from college?
    1. Physical science (i.e., physics, chemistry)
    2. Life science (i.e., biology)
    3. Social science (i.e., sociology, psychology)
    4. Humanities (i.e., English, history)
    5. Professional program (i.e., business)
    6. Engineering
    7. Mathematics
    8. Computer science

[IF Q19 = 3, 4, or 5 and Q20 = 1, 2, 6, 7, or 8]

21. What was the most important reason that you switched to this major?
    1. Took a science course that really interested me.
    2. Had a science teacher who was exceptional or who encouraged me to pursue a science major.

3. A friend who was a science major.
4. My parents or other family members encouraged me to pursue a science major.
5. It was suggested by a career counselor or career personality test.
6. I received funding/an award that prompted me to pursue a science major (please specify: ________________)
7. The job opportunities or salary.
8. I discovered that I have an aptitude for science.
9. Or was there some other reason why you switched? (please specify: ________________)

22. What was the second-most important reason that you switched to a science major?
    1. Took a science course that really interested me.
    2. Had a science teacher who was exceptional or who encouraged me to pursue a science major.
    3. A friend who was a science major.
    4. My parents or other family members encouraged me to pursue a science major.
    5. It was suggested by a career counselor or career personality test.
    6. I received funding/an award that prompted me to pursue a science major (please specify: ________________)
    7. The job opportunities or salary.
    8. I discovered that I have an aptitude for science.
    9. Or was there some other reason? (please specify: ________________)

23. As you reflect on your decision to enter the science career, were any of the following significant impediments to beginning graduate school in a science field? (select all that apply)
    1. My parents or family members did not want me to be a scientist.
    2. I was concerned I would not get a job as a scientist.
    3. My religious beliefs were in conflict with science or my religious community discouraged me from entering science.
    4. Perception that I would not fit in because of my gender.
    5. Perception that I would not fit in because of my race.

6. I was afraid that I would not be able to have a family.
7. None of the above

24. As you look back on your career so far, have any of the following kept you from progressing along the science career track as you would have liked? (select all that apply)
    1. Lack of mentoring
    2. Lack of aptitude or knowledge in my field
    3. Lack of support from family
    4. Long work hours
    5. Balancing work and family responsibilities
    6. Discrimination as a result of gender
    7. Discrimination as a result of race
    8. Lack of support from my department
    9. Lack of support from my university
    10. Lack of funding for my type of research
    11. None of the above
25. Researchers have found that there are vast differences in the proportion of women and men in different science fields. For example, there are far fewer women in physics than biology. If you were asked to give your best explanation for this difference, which one of the following comes closest to what you would hypothesize? (select ONE response)
    1. Women seem to have more natural ability in biology than in physics.
    2. Women seem to prefer biology more than physics.
    3. There is a lot more funding support for women in biology than in physics.
    4. Women are discriminated against more in physics than in biology.
    5. There are fewer mentors for women in physics than in biology.
    6. Or is there some other reason why there are fewer women in physics than in biology? (please specify: ________________)
26. In your experience, how do the men and women in your department differ in the way they balance work and family life? (select ONE response)
    1. There seems to be no difference between men and women scientists in this regard.

2. Women seem to have a lot more family responsibilities that hold them back from their professional responsibilities.
3. Women seem to have a lot more family responsibilities but these do not hold them back from their professional responsibilities.
4. Men seem to have a lot more family responsibilities that hold them back from their professional responsibilities.
5. Men seem to have a lot more family responsibilities but these do not hold them back from their professional responsibilities.
6. Or is there some other difference? (please specify: ________________)

8) No women in department.

Work and Family Responsibilities

27. Overall, how satisfied are you with your life outside the work you do at your university?
    1. Very dissatisfied
    2. Somewhat dissatisfied
    3. Neither dissatisfied nor satisfied
    4. Somewhat satisfied
    5. Very satisfied
28. Are you married or in a committed relationship?
    1. Yes, I am married
    2. Yes, I am in a committed relationship
    3. No, I do not have a spouse or partner
29. Have you ever been divorced?
    1. Yes, I have been divorced.
    2. No, I have not ever been divorced.

    [IF Q29 = 1]
30. How much do you agree or disagree with the following statement: Pursuing a career as a scientist was partly responsible for my divorce.
    1. Strongly agree
    2. Somewhat agree
    3. Have no opinion
    4. Somewhat disagree
    5. Strongly disagree

[IF Q28 = 1 or 2]

31. Do you and your spouse or partner have a commuting relationship, where one or both of you commutes to another community for work, or where you live in different communities from one another?
    1. No, my spouse/partner lives and works in the same community as me.
    2. Yes, we live together, but one or both of us commutes or travels frequently to another community for work.
    3. Yes, we live in separate communities at least part of the time.

[IF Q28 = 1 or 2]

32a. Which of the following best describes your spouse or partner's employment status?
    1. Working as a paid employee outside of academics, please specify job________________
    2. A professor in the same field
    3. A professor in another field
    4. Self-employed, independent contractor, or independent consultant
    5. Actively seeking employment
    6. Not actively seeking employment
    7. Other, please specify: ________________

[ASK IF Q32a = 6]

32b. Is he or she currently . . . (select all that apply)
    1. Caring for dependents
    2. Enrolled as a student in degree program
    3. Occupied with an unpaid internship or with volunteer activities
    4. Retired
    5. Other: ________________

33. Are you a parent or legal guardian?
    1. Yes
    2. No [SKIP TO Q37]

[IF Q33 = 1]

34. How many children have you ever had?: ________________ [IF 0, SKIP TO Q37]

[IF Q34 > 0]

35. Can you please tell me the age of your [child/children, starting with the youngest]?
    1. Age: _______
    2. Age: _______
    3. Age: _______
    4. Age: _______
    5. Age: _______
    6. Age: _______
    7. Age: _______
    8. Age: _______
    9. Age: _______
    10. Age: _______
    11. Age: _______
    12. Age: _______
    13. Age: _______
    14. Age: _______
    15. Age: _______

[IF Q34 > 0]

36. At what stage in your career were you when you had your first child?
    1. Undergraduate
    2. Graduate student
    3. Assistant professor
    4. Associate professor
    5. Full professor
    6. Other, please explain_______________
37. For the following statement, please indicate if you STRONGLY AGREE, SOMEWHAT AGREE, HAVE NO OPINION, SOMEWHAT DISAGREE or STRONGLY DISAGREE.

    I have had fewer children than I would have liked because I have pursued a career as a scientist.
    1. Strongly agree
    2. Somewhat agree
    3. Have no opinion
    4. Somewhat disagree
    5. Strongly disagree

Experiences with Discrimination

At your current university how often have you felt discriminated against based on the following:

38. Your religious beliefs?
    1. Often
    2. Sometimes
    3. Rarely
    4. Never
39. Your sexual orientation?
    1. Often
    2. Sometimes
    3. Rarely
    4. Never
40. Your racial or ethnic group?
    1. Often
    2. Sometimes
    3. Rarely
    4. Never
41. Your gender?
    1. Often
    2. Sometimes
    3. Rarely
    4. Never

Additional Demographic Questions and Other

These last few questions are for classification purposes only.

42a. Is your university salary, on a full-time basis before tax and deductions for the current year below or above $100,000?
    1. Below [GO TO 42b]
    2. Above [GO TO 42c]

42b. And, before tax and deductions, is that . . .
    1. Below $40,000
    2. $40,000–49,999
    3. $50,000–$59,999
    4. $60,000–69,999
    5. $70,000–$79,999
    6. $80,000–89,999

7. $90,000–99,999

42c. And, before tax and deductions, is that . . .

8. $100,000–109,999
9. $110,000–119,999
10. $120,000–129,999
11. $130,000–139,999
12. $140,000–149,999
13. $150,000–159,999
14. $160,000–169,999
15. $170,000–179,999
16. $180,000–189,999
17. $190,000–199,999
18. Above $200,000

43. And what is your age?

44. What is your gender?

1. Female
2. Male

45a. Just for classification purposes, are you of Hispanic origin or descent?

1. Yes
2. No

45b. What is your race? Are you White, Black, Asian, or something else?

1. White
2. Black/African American
3. Asian/Pacific Islander
5. Other (specify___________)

46. And which of the following BEST describes your US citizenship status?

1. I am a citizen of another country, not the US.
2. I was not born in the US, but I am a US citizen.
3. I was born in the US, but one of my parents was born in another country.
4. I was born in the US, but both of my parents were born in another country.
5. I was born in the US and both of my parents were born in the US.

47. What is the primary occupation that your mother (or female caregiver) held when you were age 10–16?

____

No mother/female caregiver present at that age

48. What is the primary occupation that your father (or male caregiver) held when you were age 10–16?

____

No father/male caregiver present at that age

[IF Q1 = 1 or 2]

For the following statements, please indicate if you STRONGLY AGREE, SOMEWHAT AGREE, HAVE NO OPINION, SOMEWHAT DISAGREE or STRONGLY DISAGREE.

49a. I plan to seek a tenure-track academic job at a research university.

1. Strongly agree
2. Somewhat agree
3. Have no opinion
4. Somewhat disagree
5. Strongly disagree

49b. I plan to seek a tenure-track academic job at a college or university that emphasizes teaching more than research.

1. Strongly agree
2. Somewhat agree
3. Have no opinion
4. Somewhat disagree
5. Strongly disagree

49c. I plan to seek a research scientist job in an academic setting.

1. Strongly agree
2. Somewhat agree
3. Have no opinion
4. Somewhat disagree
5. Strongly disagree

49d. I plan to seek a job as a scientist in industry.

1. Strongly agree
2. Somewhat agree
3. Have no opinion
4. Somewhat disagree
5. Strongly disagree

49e. I plan to seek a job outside of science.
1. Strongly agree
2. Somewhat agree
3. Have no opinion
4. Somewhat disagree
5. Strongly disagree

50. As we try to understand how scientists enter and remain in science it is important to understand some of the factors that lead individuals away from pursuing careers in the natural sciences. Could you recommend someone you know who left the science discipline you are currently in [at your present rank?] that you think would be interested in speaking with us about their experiences? If possible, could you also provide any contact information for these individuals?

Person 1:
Name________________
Email ________________
Phone________________

Person 2:
Name________________
Email ________________
Phone ________________

Person 3:
Name________________
Email ________________
Phone ________________

I do not have anyone to recommend

On behalf of Rice University and Southern Methodist University, thank you for participating in this survey. When the study is completed you will be provided with a summary of results. Thank you again for your time.

Appendix C

LONG INTERVIEW GUIDE

Research and Science Background

1. And in a few sentences, could you describe the general topic or questions you address in your central research? [*Note: The respondents will often spend a lot of time talking about this, so it's good to have in mind how to help them move to the next question and not to ask too many follow-up questions to this one.*]
2. To start, could you describe briefly how you decided to become a [*insert biologist or physicist*]? [*PROBE: Specifically, were there experiences that you had or people that you encountered who were important in helping you decide to be a scientist? Note: Be hesitant to use this probe, however, as we do not want to put ideas in their mind about people or experiences that are not there.*]

Family, Primary, Secondary, Undergraduate Educational Experiences

3. How about your family? Did your parents/caregivers play any role (if so, what?) in your decision to be a scientist?
4. How about your grade school or high school experiences? Were there any particular experiences/people in grade school or high school that influenced your decision to enter science?
5. What was your major as an undergraduate and could you actually tell me where you did your undergraduate work [*try to ask about undergraduate institution in a casual way*]?
6. Could you tell me a little about how you decided to major in [*insert major*]?
7. What were some of the important influences on your choice of specific undergraduate major [*PROBE: such as people or experiences*]?
8. [*Note: If switched to a science major after being in another type of major, if not SKIP*] Could you tell me the story of why you decided to switch to being a science major?

Decision-Making for Jobs

9. How about the choice of field to major in in graduate school? What were some of the important influences in your choice to go to graduate school in physics [*PROBE: such as people or experiences*]?
10. [*If in a faculty position*] Did you do a postdoctoral fellowship? How about your postdoctoral fellowship? How did you come to choose this particular postdoctoral opportunity? What were some of the important influences on this choice?
11. [*If in a postdoctoral fellowship*] How did you come to choose this particular postdoctoral opportunity? What were some of the important influences on this choice?
12. [*If in a faculty position*] How did you come to this particular faculty position? What were some of the important influences on this choice?
13. [*If a graduate student or postdoctoral fellow*] Could you tell me a little about your career plans for after you finish your [*graduate degree/postdoctoral fellowship*]?

Challenges Faced in Science Career (General, University, Department)

I am going to switch now to talking a little about the challenges you have faced as a scientist.

14. Thinking over the past stages of your career as a scientist, could you tell me a little about the one or two most significant challenges that you have faced in continuing your career as a scientist? [*If possible try and probe the respondent for the most significant challenge.*]
15. How about issues related to discrimination? Have there been any particular difficulties in your science career so far related to discrimination? If there have been, could you tell me the story of one incident that affected you in particular? [*It's important here not to supply the forms of discrimination for the respondent or give them leading examples; we are interested in what the respondent thinks of as discrimination.*]
16. What about others' stories of discrimination? Have you known of others in your department or broader field who have experienced discrimination? Could you tell me a little bit about their stories?

17. If there are any, could you talk a little about some of the challenges you might face in your particular department as related to your career as a scientist? And related, are there particular things about your department that are useful/helpful to your career as a scientist?
18. How about in your broader university? Are there specific challenges you face in your broader university related to pursuing your career as a scientist? And are there things that are particularly helpful that you want to mention?

Family and Career

19. Do you have children? [*If respondent has children*] Could you tell me a little about what it has been like to raise children while maintaining your career as a scientist? Have there been any particular challenges in your career?
20. [*If respondent does not have children*] How do you think a career in science might have an impact on your family choices?
21. Do you think that you have fewer children than you might have had if you had not been a scientist? [*Note: If yes, ask respondent to extrapolate on this answer.*]
22. [*If has children*] Could you tell me about your next career step and how having children might factor into your next career move, if you think it does at all?
23. [*If have children*] How do you think it is different being an academic parent or a parent who is a scientist when compared to a parent with a different kind of job?
24. [*Asked of all respondents with children*] Do you think that having children is difficult to manage with being a scientist? Why or why not?
25. [*Asked of women who have children*] Could you compare your experience of having children and being a scientist to the experiences of your male colleagues who have children? Do you think you face any unique challenges?

Tenure Achievement

26. From what you know about other disciplines, how would you compare the difficulty in achieving a tenure-track position in your discipline when say, compared to [*insert biology or physics*]? Do you think

there are any unique challenges in achieving a tenure-track faculty position in your discipline when compared to other disciplines?

27. [*If faculty member and untenured*] How about achieving tenure? What do you think are the possibilities for achieving tenure in your field and in your particular department?
28. [*If tenured*] Could you describe a little of what it was like for you to achieve tenure? Did you get tenure in this particular department? [*If yes*] Were there any unique challenges that you faced in achieving tenure in this department? [*If no*] Were there any unique challenges that you faced in achieving tenure in the department where you received tenure?

Time Management and Scholarly Productivity
Now some questions about your time and how your personal life and work life fit together.

29. To what extent do your responsibilities outside of work influence the work you do as a scientist?
30. How about your work time? To what extent do you feel like you have ownership over your work time?
31. To what extent do you feel that you are as productive in your research as you would like? Why or why not?
32. [*If respondent said not as productive as they would like, then ask*] What is holding you back from being more productive?

Job Satisfaction

33. Overall how satisfied are you with your life outside the work you do at your university? Could you tell me a little bit about why [*you are not satisfied/are satisfied*]?
34. Have you ever thought about making a transition at this point in your career track to a career outside of academic science? To what extent do you think you might pursue this at some point? [*If says will never pursue this*] What is holding you back from pursuing another type of career?
35. [*If graduate student or postdoctoral fellow*] Could you tell me a little about your future career plans for after you graduate/finish this position? [*If remarks that wants to have an academic position*] Specifically, could you tell me what kind of academic position and what kind of university you would hope to work in?

Biology and Physics Differences

36. Researchers have found that there are vast differences in the proportion of women and men in different science fields. For example, there are far fewer women in physics than biology. If you were asked to give your best explanation for this difference, what would be your explanation?

Public Science Issues

37. I wonder if you are involved in any work aimed at translating science to individuals outside the academy or the scientific community? Could you tell me a little about these efforts?
38. Do you think scientists in general are doing a good enough job at translating science to broader communities? Why or why not?
39. [*If no to above*] How could they be doing a better job?

Basic Demographics

40. Just for the record, could I ask some questions about your demographics?
41. What is your academic rank or place in your career? [*Note: If you think you already know the answer to this question, then say something like, "You are an assistant professor, right?"*]
42. How old are you?
43. How would you describe your ethnic group?
44. Are you married or in a long-term partnership?
45. How long have you been married [*try to find out if first or second or more marriage*]?
46. If so, what does your spouse do for their work?
47. Does your spouse work in the same city?
48. [*If in a commuting relationship*] Maybe you could tell me a little about how living in a different city than your spouse influences your work.
49. [*If respondent has children from earlier question, try to find out gender of children and how many.*] What are their ages?

At this point I want to ask again if there are any specific questions that you have for me? Are there things that we have not covered?

NOTES

CHAPTER 1. WHEN NOTHING MATTERS EXCEPT SCIENCE

1 Phys51F, conducted 10/28/10. We include here the respondent code, date of interview, and some demographic information.
2 Weber, *The Methodology of the Social Sciences.*
3 Phys60M, conducted 11/19/10.
4 Cech et al., "Professional Role Confidence," 641–66.
5 Hermanowicz, *The Stars Are Not Enough.*
6 Blair-Loy, *Competing Devotions.*
7 See ibid. See also Whyte, *The Organization Man.*
8 Cooper, "Being the 'Go-to Guy,'" 379–405.
9 See Bielby and Bielby, "Work Commitment," 234–47; Blair-Loy, *Competing Devotions*; Cooper, "Being the 'Go-to Guy'"; and Epstein et al., *The Part-Time Paradox.*
10 See Jacobs and Gerson, *The Time Divide*; and Misra, Lundquist, and Templer, "Gender, Work Time, and Care Responsibilities," 300–323.
11 Ecklund and Lincoln, "Scientists Want More Children," e22590.
12 Keller, "The Origin, History, and Politics," 80–94.
13 Coser, *Greedy Institutions.*
14 Hermanowicz, *The Stars Are Not Enough*, 153.
15 Gibbons et al., *The New Production of Knowledge.*
16 See Fox, "Women and Scientific Careers," 205–24; and Shapin, *The Scientific Life.*
17 See Gerson, *The Unfinished Revolution*; Hochschild and Machung, *The Second Shift*; and Williams, *Unbending Gender.*
18 Mason, Goulden, and Frasch, "Keeping Women in the Science Pipeline."
19 Aumann, Galinsky, and Matos, *The New Male Mystique.*
20 Parker and Wang, "Modern Parenthood."
21 See Gornick and Meyers, *Families That Work.*
22 See Zuo, "The Effect of Men's Breadwinner Status," 799–816; and Gerson, *No Man's Land.*
23 See Hochschild and Machung, *The Second Shift*; Moen and Roehling, *The Career Mystique*; and Cha, "Reinforcing Separate Spheres," 303–29.
24 Folbre, *Valuing Children.*
25 There is an established literature on how dual-career academic couples negotiate finding jobs and maintaining jobs at the same academic institution, only some of which we mention here. See, for example, Wolf-Wendel, Twombly, and Rice,

"Dual Career Couples," 291–321; Ferber and Loeb, *Academic Couples*; and Didion, "Dual Careers and Shared Positions," 123–24.

26 DiMaggio and Powell, "The Iron Cage Revisited," 147–160.

27 See Douglas, *How Institutions Think*; and Coser, *Greedy Institutions*.

28 Mason, Goulden, and Frasch, "Keeping Women in the Science Pipeline."

29 See Rosser and Taylor, "Why Are We Still Worried," 7–10; and Mason and Goulden, "Marriage and Baby Blues," 86–103.

30 Rosser and Taylor, "Why Are We Still Worried," 7–10.

31 Our research shows that job satisfaction—how scientists feel about their work lives—is strongly predictive of their satisfaction with life *outside* of work.

32 Hirschman, *Exit, Voice, and Loyalty*.

33 Preston, "Plugging the Leaks," 69–74.

34 In comparison, only 18 percent responded to Van Anders's survey of science graduate students ("Why the Academic Pipeline Leaks"); Preston's study of retention and exit from science careers received a 35 percent response (*Leaving Science*); and even the highly successful Carnegie Commission study of faculty resulted in only a 59.8 percent response (Martin, *Technical Report*).

35 See England et al., "Why Are Some Academic Fields Tipping toward Female?," 23–42; and McDonnell, "Why So Few Choose Physics," 583–86.

36 Life sciences figures from "Table 5-15: SEH Doctorate Holders Employed in Academia, by Type of Position, Sex, and Degree Field, 1973–2010" from National Science Board, *Science and Engineering Indicators 2014* (NSB 14-01), http://www.nsf.gov/statistics/seind14/content/chapter-5/at05-15.pdf. The NSF does not distinguish between physics and other physical sciences, which overrepresents women as comprising 21 percent of a broader category consisting of physical science faculty; thus, physics figures are from the American Institute of Physics. Women constitute 19 percent of faculty in astronomy degree–granting departments. "Women among Physics & Astronomy Faculty: Results from the 2010 Survey of Physics Degree–Granting Departments," https://www.aip.org/sites/default/files/statistics/faculty/womenfac-pa-10.pdf.

37 See Leslie et al., "Expectations of Brilliance," 262–65.

38 British sociologists Tony Becher and Paul Trowler talk about the culture of academic disciplines in *Academic Tribes and Territories*.

39 Dye, *Top Down Policymaking*.

40 See Lindsay, *Faith in the Halls of Power*; and Fox, "Women and Men Faculty in Academic Science and Engineering," 997–1012.

41 Rosser and Taylor, "Why Are We Still Worried."

42 See Nippert-Eng, *Home and Work*, which focuses on industrial scientists. See also Smith-Doerr, *Women's Work*.

43 Bio15F, conducted 07/27/09.

44 Bio52F, conducted 06/07/10.

CHAPTER 2. FAMILY MATTERS TO SCIENCE

1 Phys50F, conducted 08/31/10.
2 Bio22M, conducted 07/31/09.
3 Bio25F, conducted 08/07/09.
4 Bio49F, conducted 05/24/10.
5 Phys50F, conducted 08/31/10.
6 Bio15F, conducted 07/14/09.
7 Mason, Wolfinger, and Goulden, *Do Babies Matter?*
8 Bio17M, conducted 07/28/09.
9 Bio11F, conducted 07/15/09.
10 Bio49F, conducted 05/24/10.
11 For more of the nuances of this debate, see Risman, *Families as They Really Are.*
12 For example, see Moen and Yu, "Effective Work/Life Strategies," 291–326. See also Schieman and Glavin, "Trouble at the Border?," 590–611.
13 See Edgell, *Religion and Family in a Changing Society*, 28–29.
14 See Schieman, Milkie, and Glavin, "When Work Interferes with Life," 966–88.
15 See Zuckerman, "Stratification in American Science," 235–57, who discusses the ways in which current gender stratification in science may be linked to "male" notions of power structures. See also Gieryn, "Boundary-Work and the Demarcation of Science from Non-science," 781–95, who discusses the "problem of demarcation: how to identify unique and essential characteristics of science that distinguish it from other kinds of intellectual activities" (781).
16 This is what some sociologists of gender and science have called a "male way" of thinking about the world of work. See Kelly, "The Construction of Masculine Science," 133–54. According to Kelly, "Men's involvement in their work lives, sometimes to the exclusion of all else, has been frequently noted. This article explores the unique relationship men have with their work. Drawing on concepts from anthropological research and psychoanalytic theory, it considers some of the developmental roots of men's intense feelings about their work. Special emphasis is placed on the ego ideal as an organizing concept at the interface of culture and individual personality that helps clarify a man's relationship to his work. A case example and treatment considerations show how men's passion about their work can be both a progressive force in their lives and a source of marked vulnerability that can be a focus of therapy" (133).
17 Bio76M, conducted 08/26/10.
18 Bio18M, conducted 07/29/09.
19 In 2010, women constituted 46.7 percent of the labor force, up from 42.5 percent in 1980 and 38.1 percent in 1970 (Bureau of Labor Statistics, "Table 2"). By 2009, wives' earnings contributed 37.1 percent of households' earnings, up from 26.7 percent in 1980 (Bureau of Labor Statistics, "Table 24").
20 Among married couples in which both spouses work, 28.9 percent of wives earned more than their husbands in 2009 (Bureau of Labor Statistics, "Table 25").

21 Coltrane, "Elite Careers and Family Commitment," 214–20.
22 National Institutes of Health, "Research Project Grants."
23 American Institute of Physics, "Women among Physics & Astronomy Faculty: Results from the 2010 Survey of Physics Degree–Granting Departments," 2013, https://www.aip.org/sites/default/files/statistics/faculty/womenfac-pa-10.pdf.
24 National Science Foundation, "Graduate Enrollment in S&E Fields."
25 National Academy of Sciences, National Academy of Engineering, and Institute of Medicine of the National Academies, *Beyond Bias and Barriers.*
26 See England et al., "Why Are Some Academic Fields Tipping toward Female?," 23–42. See also Xie and Shauman, *Women in Science.*
27 Van Anders, "Why the Academic Pipeline Leaks," 511–21.
28 Taylor, "Occupational Sex Composition," 189–212.
29 Mennino and Brayfield, "Job-Family Trade-offs," 226–56.
30 Ducharme and Martin, "Unrewarding Work," 223–43.
31 See Moen and Yu, "Effective Work/Life Strategies." See also Hill et al., "A Cross-Cultural Test," 1300–1316.
32 See Schieman and Glavin, "Trouble at the Border?" See also Schieman, Milkie, and Glavin, "When Work Interferes with Life," 966–88.
33 Glass and Estes, "The Family Responsive Workplace," 289–313.
34 Keen and Quadagno, "Predictors of Perceived Work-Family Balance," 1–23.
35 See England, *Comparable Worth.* See also Frehill, "Education and Occupational Sex Segregation," 225–49.
36 See Hakim, "Lifestyle Preferences as Determinants," 428–59. See also Polachek, "How the Life-Cycle Human Capital Model Explains Why the Gender Wage Gap Narrowed," 102–24.
37 Preston, *Leaving Science.*
38 See Xie and Shauman, *Women in Science.* See also Zuckerman, Cole, and Bruer, *The Outer Circle.*
39 Preston, *Leaving Science.*
40 Respondent ID 1120, question 26.
41 Damaske et al., "Male Scientists' Competing Devotions," 477–507.
42 Respondent ID 424, question 26.
43 Respondent ID 1381, question 26.
44 Respondent ID 1457, question 26.
45 Bio11F, conducted 07/15/09.
46 Phys26F, conducted 04/02/10.
47 Respondent ID 1013, question 26.
48 Phys45F, conducted 06/07/10.
49 Thirty-four percent of male biologists vs. 26 percent of male physicists and 41 percent of female biologists vs. 33 percent of female physicists report that their careers have suffered from trying to balance work and family responsibilities.
50 Phys41M, conducted 05/24/10.
51 Bio6F, conducted 06/19/09.

52 Bio28F, conducted 08/25/09.
53 "Supply Side Academics," 1337.
54 Phys51F, conducted 10/28/10.
55 Bio17M, conducted 07/28/09.
56 Bio41M, conducted 04/09/10.
57 Bio18M, conducted 07/29/09.
58 Bio24F, conducted 08/06/09.
59 Phys40M, conducted 05/24/10.
60 Phys63F, conducted 11/29/10.
61 Bio47F, conducted 04/28/10.
62 Bio24F, conducted 08/06/09.
63 Phys17M, conducted 02/09/10.

CHAPTER 3. WILL I MAKE IT?

1 Phys 50F, conducted 08/31/10.
2 See Fox, "Gender, Family Characteristics, and Publication Productivity," 131–50; Fox, Fonseca, and Bao, "Work and Family Conflict in Academic Science," 715–35; and Long, "Discussion."
3 Bio22M, conducted 07/31/09.
4 Nerad and Cerny, "Postdoctoral Patterns," 1533–535.
5 "Supply Side Academics," 1337.
6 Cyranoski et al., "Education," 276–79; see also Bardin, "For Science Ph.D.'s."
7 Phys51F, conducted 10/28/10.
8 Phys3F, conducted 06/09/11.
9 The data presented in figures 3.1 and 3.2 and in all tables are from our "Influences on Science Career" survey, conducted in 2009.
10 Phys2F, conducted 06/10/09.
11 Preston, "Plugging the Leaks," 69–74.
12 See, for example, Shauman and Xie, "Geographic Mobility of Scientists," 455–68.
13 See Cole and Zuckerman, "Marriage, Motherhood and Research Performance," 125.
14 Phys47M, conducted 07/08/10.
15 See Mason, Wolfinger, and Golden, *Do Babies Matter?*
16 Bio70F, conducted 08/10/10.
17 Phys29F, conducted 04/15/10.
18 Phys22M, conducted 02/11/10.
19 Phys2F, conducted 06/10/09.
20 Phys3F, conducted 06/11/09.
21 The NSF funds a mere 10 percent of received applications, and the National Institutes of Health funds only 15 percent of the applications received in 2011. See National Institutes of Health, "Research Project Grants."
22 Edin and Nelson, *Doing the Best I Can.*

23 Forty-nine percent of employed men with families reported experiencing some or a lot of work-family conflict in 2008, compared with 24 percent in 1977 ($p < .001$). See Aumann, Galinsky, and Matos, *The New Male Mystique*, 2.
24 Bio2M, conducted 06/09/09.
25 Bio22M, conducted 07/31/09.
26 Bio3M, conducted 06/09/09.
27 Bio12M, conducted 07/16/09.
28 Unique ID 13407 female graduate student in physics.
29 Phys2F, conducted 06/10/09.
30 Bio58F, conducted 07/12/10.
31 Bio63F, conducted 07/28/10.
32 Bio69F, conducted 08/10/10.
33 Phys3F, conducted 06/11/09.
34 Bio64F, conducted 07/29/10.
35 Bio60F, conducted 07/21/10.
36 $p = .0000$, $n = 684$.
37 $p = .0384$, $n = 504$.
38 $p < .0001$, $n = 472$.
39 $p = .7379$, $n = 639$.
40 $p = .2790$, $n = 463$.
41 See Hirschman, *Exit, Voice, and Loyalty*.
42 Phys46F, conducted 05/25/10.
43 Bio70F, conducted 08/10/10.
44 Phys11M, conducted 02/02/10.

CHAPTER 4. MANAGING THE CONTROLLED CRASH

1 Phys64M, conducted 03/29/11.
2 Bio52F, conducted 06/07/10.
3 See Harrington, *Career Management and Work-Life Integration*.
4 For information on work-family tensions across professions, see Hochschild and Machung, *The Second Shift*; Moen, *Women's Two Roles*; and Williams, *Unbending Gender*. For other work on gender, science, and fertility, see Wolfinger, Mason, and Goulden, "Problems in the Pipeline," 388–405.
5 See Xie and Shauman, *Women in Science*. See also Zuckerman, Cole, and Bruer, *The Outer Circle*.
6 Phys13M, conducted 02/04/10.
7 Martinez et al., "Fertility, Contraception, and Fatherhood." According to this study, 25.1 years is the mean age when a first child is born to men aged 15 to 44 who have ever fathered a biological child.
8 See Moen and Roehling, *The Career Mystique*. See also Bianchi, Robinson, and Milkie, *Changing Rhythms of American Family Life*.
9 See Glauber, "Gender and Race in Families and at Work," 8–30.

10 See Maume, "Gender Differences in Restricting Work Efforts," 859–69; Astone et al., "Men's Work Efforts," 3–13; and Lundberg and Rose, "Parenthood and the Earnings of Married Men and Women," 689–710.

11 Thirty-seven out of 150 of those interviewed have a spouse who is also a scientist. In pointing out the ways both men and women scientists struggle to be scientist parents, we do not want to in any way de-emphasize the problems with discrimination that women in academic science still face and that mothers face in particular, especially those struggles faced by many women who will not end up at the top research universities we studied; the difficulties of balancing science careers with having children may well keep them out of science. We will turn to these realities in the next chapter.

12 Phys34F, conducted 04/29/10.

13 See Hermanowicz, *Lives in Science*; Blair-Loy, *Competing Devotions*; and Whyte, *The Organization Man*.

14 See Acker, "Hierarchies, Jobs, and Bodies," 139–58; Whyte, *The Organization Man*; and Williams, *Unbending Gender*.

15 See Williams, *Unbending Gender*. See also Becker, *Treatise on the Family*.

16 See DiMaggio, "Culture and Cognition," 263–88. See also Blair-Loy, *Competing Devotions*.

17 See Cooper, "Being the 'Go-to Guy,'" 379–405.

18 See ibid. See also Hochschild, *The Time Bind*.

19 See Jacobs and Gerson, *The Time Divide*.

20 See Patten and Parker, "A Gender Reversal on Career Aspirations."

21 See Shapin, *The Scientific Life*. See also Latour and Woolgar, *Laboratory Life*.

22 See Nippert-Eng, *Home and Work*, for a description of the physical practices workers employ to construct boundaries between home and work.

23 Phys26F, conducted 04/05/10.

24 These figures come primarily from qualitative interview data. The survey cannot distinguish a spouse at the same prestige level, but it does identify that, among married faculty, 29.8 percent of men and 58.4 percent of women have an academic spouse. Expanded to those who are not married but are in committed relationships, those figures are 30.3 percent for women and 57.1 percent for men.

25 See Shauman and Xie, "Geographic Mobility of Scientists," 455–68.

26 Table 3.3 shows living apart and commuting status by career stage.

27 Phys7F, conducted 08/06/09.

28 Phys61F, conducted 11/19/10.

29 Bio21F, conducted 07/30/09.

30 Bio75M, conducted 08/20/10.

31 Phys30F, conducted 04/21/10.

32 Bio72F, conducted 08/11/10.

33 Bio20M, conducted 07/30/09.

34 In some cases, for both scientists to succeed, they have to look for jobs in different places and decide to live apart. In our survey, 45 percent of the scientists who live apart have children. An associate professor in her early forties, whose husband works in business in another state, says living separately from her husband has sometimes been frustrating and personally difficult, and "getting someone to take care of the kids" has been the biggest problem.
35 Bio13F, conducted 07/16/09.
36 Bio33F, conducted 02/04/10.
37 Phys9F, conducted 08/31/09.
38 59.1 hours for women and 57.8 hours for men ($p = .4219$, $n = 369$).
39 $p = .5742$, $n = 912$.
40 See Jacobs and Winslow, "Overworked Faculty," 104–29.
41 Bio10M, conducted 07/14/09.
42 Bio33F, conducted 02/04/10.
43 Bio21F, conducted 07/30/09.
44 $p < .0000$, $n = 1{,}302$.
45 1.2 children for women vs. 1.5 for men.
46 Bio78F, conducted 10/06/10.
47 Phys32F, conducted 04/26/10.
48 Bio17M, conducted 07/28/09.
49 Phys39M, conducted 05/18/10.
50 Bio49F, conducted 05/24/10; Phys26F, conducted 04/05/10.
51 Phys26F, conducted 04/05/10. See the following for more context for this quote: "So the way it works now the kids are in school and of course it's much easier now they are five and eight, and he picks them up every day at three o'clock, so he drops them off and he picks them up, so he gets to work on his music from eight to three, he picks them up, and then I get home, not too late, like five or six, and we have the evening together and then I'm exhausted and go to sleep and he does a couple more hours of music. But I think that women I see who are married to professionals, in any field, have a, unless they simply buy child care for ten hours a day, and accept that, which is fine, unless they are happy with that, I think it's really really hard, and I think, my understanding from research from your sort of field is that many women leave because of this issue, and I think that's true across many professions. So I really feel that the part of why I have been able to be successful is because I've got a spouse who is doing at this point more than 50 percent of the child care."
52 Bio49F, conducted 05/24/10.
53 Phys32F, conducted 04/26/10.
54 Bio27M, conducted 08/11/09.
55 Phys56M, conducted 11/08/10.
56 For more information on cognitive schema, see DiMaggio, "Culture and Cognition," 263–88.
57 Bio4M, conducted 06/10/09.

58 Phys52F, conducted 10/18/10.

59 This mirrors broader research that shows "46 percent of fathers feel they spend too little time with children, compared with 23 percent of mothers." See Parker and Wang, "Modern Parenthood."

60 Phys52F, conducted 10/28/10.

61 Bio81F, conducted 10/14/10.

62 Phys26F, conducted 04/05/10.

63 Phys52F, conducted 10/28/10.

64 Phys40M, conducted 05/24/10.

65 Bio82F, conducted 11/01/10.

66 Phys57M, conducted 11/10/10.

67 Bio21F, conducted 07/30/09.

68 Bio53F, conducted 06/08/10.

69 Bio50M, conducted 05/24/10.

70 Phys56M, conducted 11/08/10.

71 Bio10M, conducted 07/15/09.

72 According to Lingston and Cohn, "Childlessness Up among All Women; Down among Women with Advanced Degrees."

73 We used logistic regression in these analyses. We adjusted for sex, age, rank, income, marital status, number of children, weekly hours worked, scholarly productivity, and satisfaction with life outside work.

CHAPTER 5. WHEN THE IDEAL SCIENTIST MEETS THE IDEAL MOTHER

1 Phys2F, conducted 06/10/09.

2 Bio68F, conducted 08/10/10.

3 See Hakim, "Lifestyle Preferences as Determinants," 428–59. See also Polachek, "How the Life-Cycle Human Capital Model Explains Why the Gender Wage Gap Narrowed," 102–24.

4 See Fox, "Women and Scientific Careers," 205–24; Hochschild and Machung, *The Second Shift*; Moen, *Women's Two Roles*; Shapin, *The Scientific Life*; and Williams, *Unbending Gender*.

5 Statistically women have 1.2 children, compared with 1.5 for men, $p < .0000$, $n = 1{,}297$.

6 From our survey this was 45.4 percent of women, compared with 24.5 percent of men ($p < .0000$, $n = 1{,}302$).

7 This is 15.5 percent of women vs. 11.5 percent of men ($p = .0438$, $n = 1{,}302$).

8 This is exactly 59.1 hours for women and 57.8 hours for men ($p = .4219$, $n = 369$).

9 This is exactly 54.5 hours for women and 53.9 hours for men ($p = .5742$, $n = 912$). Also keep in mind that these are scientists who have made it to the elite research university level.

10 See Hays, *The Cultural Contradictions of Motherhood.*

11 Damaske and Gerson, "Viewing 21st Century Motherhood," 233–48.

12 Bio81F, conducted 10/14/10.
13 Phys26F, conducted 04/05/10.
14 Bio43F, conducted 04/20/10.
15 World Bank, "Fertility Rate, Total."
16 "United States," CIA World Fact Book.
17 Bio64F, conducted 07/29/10.
18 Bio15F, conducted 07/27/09.
19 Bio49F, conducted 05/24/10.
20 See Artis, "Breastfeed at Your Own Risk"; Rippeyoung and Noonan, "Is Breast-feeding Truly Cost Free?," 244–67; U.S. Department of Health and Human Services, Office on Women's Health, "HHS Blueprint for Action on Breastfeeding"; and Orit, "Five Myths about Breast-feeding."
21 Artis, "Breastfeed at Your Own Risk."
22 Phys52F, conducted 10/28/10.
23 Bio78F, conducted 10/06/10.
24 Bio70F, conducted 08/10/10.
25 Ibid.
26 Bio70F, conducted 08/10/10.
27 Bio13F, conducted 07/16/10.
28 Bio49F conducted 05/24/10.
29 Bio32F, conducted 09/04/09.
30 Phys26F, conducted 04/02/10.
31 Bio47F, conducted 04/28/10.
32 54.5 hours for women and 53.9 hours for men, $p = .5742$, $n = 912$.
33 Bio47F, conducted 04/28/10.
34 Bio11F, conducted 07/15/09.
35 See Coontz, *The Way We Never Were*; Moen and Roehling, *The Career Mystique*; and Williams and Boushey, "The Three Faces of Work-Family Conflict."
36 Hays, *The Cultural Contradictions of Motherhood.*
37 Phys26F, conducted 04/02/10.
38 Bio45F, conducted 04/23/10.
39 Bio81F, conducted 10/14/10.
40 Bio72F, conducted 08/11/10.
41 Bio33F, conducted 02/04/10.
42 Bio52F, conducted 06/07/10.
43 This statistic results from a search for the words "luck" or "lucky" in each interview transcript of scientists with children or those who anticipate having children in the immediate future. Counts were collected for each of these words and separated by male or female, then divided by the total number of scientists in these categories in each gender (NTOTALMALE = 37; NTOTALFEMALE = 35; NLUCKFEMALE = 12).
44 Phys46F, conducted 05/25/10.
45 Bio21F, conducted 07/30/09.
46 Coontz, *The Way We Never Were.*

47 Bio43F, conducted 04/20/10.

48 See Hochschild, *The Managed Heart*, who discusses the way in which—especially in professional roles—workers bridge a gap between what we feel and what we "ought" to feel in our particular role; we take guidance from "feeling rules" that are socially constructed by our professional worlds as well as the broader society.

49 Phys52F, conducted 10/28/10.

50 Bio82F, conducted 11/01/10.

51 Bio52F, conducted 06/07/10.

52 Bio21F, conducted 07/30/09.

53 Ibid.

54 Bio10M, conducted 07/14/09.

55 Bio21F, conducted 07/30/09.

56 Bio68F, conducted 08/10/10.

57 Bio49F, conducted 05/24/10.

58 Phys32F, conducted 04/26/10.

59 Bio15F, conducted 07/14/09.

60 Bio78F, conducted 10/06/10.

61 See Blau, "Expertise and Power in Professional Organization," 102–23; Kanter, *Men and Women of the Corporation*; see also Williams, *Gender Differences at Work*; and Williams, *Still a Man's World*.

62 Blalock, *Toward a Theory of Minority-Group Relations*.

63 See, for example, Taylor, "Occupational Sex Composition," 189–212.

64 Wall and Arnold, "How Involved Is Involved Fathering," 508–27.

65 Phys48F, conducted 07/22/10.

66 Phys52F, conducted 10/28/10.

67 Phys48F, conducted 07/22/10.

68 See Becker, *Treatise on the Family*.

69 See Hays, *The Cultural Contradictions of Motherhood*. In particular see chapter 7, "Love, Self-Interest, Power, and Opposition: Untangling the Roots of Intensive Mothering."

70 Bio78F, conducted 10/06/10.

71 Bio21F, conducted 07/30/09.

72 See Folbre, *The Invisible Heart*, for a discussion of this phenomenon.

73 Phys24F, conducted 03/16/10.

74 Bio78F, conducted 10/06/10.

75 Bio24F, conducted 06/08/09.

76 Bio78F, conducted 10/06/10.

CHAPTER 6. A WAY FORWARD FOR UNIVERSITIES, SCIENCE, AND SCIENTISTS

1 Bio52F, conducted 06/07/10.

2 See, in particular, Stewart, McMalley, and LaVaque-Manty, *Transforming Science and Engineering*. See also Demos, Berheide, and Segal, *Advances in Gender Research*.

3 See DiMaggio and Powell, "The Iron Cage Revisited," 147–60.
4 See Mason, Goulden, and Frasch, "Keeping Women in the Science Pipeline."
5 Maldonado and La Salle, "Dear Colleague Letter."
6 http://www.nsf.gov/pubs/2010/nsf10593/nsf10593.htm. These grants to individual research institutions have done many good things, encouraging universities to take seriously the gender stratification at all stages of the science and engineering career. The program—which we benefit from greatly in our analyses—tends to focus mainly on understanding and bringing change to an individual institution rather than analyzing data across university contexts. And such programs tend to neglect the lives of men.
7 See Kerber, "We Must Make the Academic Workplace More Humane and Equitable," B6–B9. See also Drago et al., "Faculty and Families Project."
8 See "Fathers/Program Helps Dads Deal with Stress."
9 See Owens et al., "Data from the 2012 Working Mother 100 Best Companies."
10 See Smith-Doerr, *Women's Work*. See also Whittington and Smith-Doerr, "Women Inventors in Context," 194–218.
11 See, for example, Greenwood and Levin, "Re-organizing Universities," 433–40, who discuss the hierarchical aspects of university life, as well as the ways in which universities are resistant to change.
12 Bio13F, conducted 07/16/09.
13 Phys2F, conducted 06/10/09.
14 Bio21F, conducted 07/30/09.
15 Of the 150 respondents we interviewed, 39 respondents mentioned it (26 percent), and just about 33 percent of respondents with children mentioned it, but actually a good amount *without children* mentioned it.
16 Bio12M, conducted 07/16/09.
17 Phys8M, conducted 08/24/09.
18 "The Child Care Tuition Assistance Program (CCTAP) for UW-Madison Students."
19 Geiger, *To Advance Knowledge*.
20 At least one center in the Harvard University day care bases fees on a sliding scale, but the lowest rung is anything below $72,686 for the total household gross income, and the application includes the following note: "Families whose gross income is at Level 1 are subject to a comprehensive financial review and eligibility process. We have limited funds to subsidize families at this level." Thus, families at that income level have to go through a separate application.
21 "Whatever you choose, you should know that affordable, high-quality child-care is in short supply in the greater Boston area. Affiliation with Harvard University does not guarantee admission to Harvard-affiliated child-care centers. You increase your odds for securing the type of child care you want if you start looking early. It's a good idea to visit and apply to child care centers as much as one year in advance. Family day care and in-home care may require less lead time, but will require an intensive process of identifying and reviewing your options." From "Child Care," Harvard University.

22 Bio21F, conducted 07/30/09.
23 Bio27M, conducted 08/11/09.
24 Bio30F, conducted 08/27/09.
25 Phys52F, conducted 10/28/10.
26 Phys26F, conducted 04/05/10. Significantly, recent census statistics show 25 percent of American households have a woman as the primary breadwinner.
27 Anderson, "American University Professor."
28 Baer and Van Ummersen, "An Agenda for Excellence," 6.
29 Respondent ID 2714, question 26, in response to an open-ended survey question.
30 The following is found on the NSF website: "Can NSF award funds be used for travel and associated dependent-care expenses for dependents of individuals funded on an NSF award? NSF award funds may not be used for domestic travel costs or associated dependent-care expenses for individuals traveling on NSF award funds. Travel costs associated with dependents may be allowable for international travel in accordance with Award and Administration Guide Chapter V.B.4, which contains several stipulations, including that travel must be continuous for a period of six months or more. Can conference/workshop awards or travel funds from research awards be used to support child care at conferences and workshops? NSF award funds may not be used to pay for travel costs or expenses related to onsite care (e.g., day care) for dependents of participants at NSF-sponsored conferences and workshops. NSF-sponsored conferences and workshops are encouraged to consider child-care services to ease the burden on attendees, but the costs of such services are the responsibility of those that choose to utilize the accommodations." See National Science Foundation, "US NSF—Frequently Asked Questions Related to Dependent Care—nsf10032."
31 Phys2F, conducted 06/10/09.
32 Bio70F, conducted 08/10/10.
33 We want to mention the work of other scholars who have outlined changes that need to be made in university tenure policies in order for universities to better support families. See, for example, Baer and Van Ummersen, "An Agenda for Excellence."
34 Bio66M, conducted 08/09/10.
35 Bio25F, conducted 08/07/09.
36 Phys46F, conducted 05/25/10.
37 Phys52F, conducted 10/28/10.
38 Bio60F, conducted 07/21/10.
39 Phys13M, conducted 02/04/10.
40 Phys15M, conducted 02/04/10.
41 See again Stewart, McMalley, and LaVaque-Manty, *Transforming Science and Engineering*. See especially "Thread 5. *Removal of subtle gender, racial, and other biases in promotion and tenure*" (284–85). A "Promotion and Tenure ADVANCE Committee (PTAC)" was appointed to evaluate the tenure system and report any possible biases, including those based on gender (285).

42 Bio32F, conducted 09/04/09.
43 Phys24F, conducted 03/16/10.
44 Phys12M, conducted 02/03/10.
45 Bio26M, conducted 08/10/09.
46 Bio81F, conducted 10/08/10.
47 Phys57M, conducted 11/10/10.
48 Phys11M, conducted 02/02/10.
49 Phys2F, conducted 06/10/09.
50 Institutional theorists argue that individuals more readily accept one cognitive schema (way of interpreting the world) when it is bundled with another cognitive schema that they find acceptable. See DiMaggio, "Culture and Cognition," 263–87. See also Long, "Stories as Carriers of Theory," who, in a 2007 address to the sociology of culture miniconference held as part of the American Sociological Association, discussed the importance of stories as vehicles of central theoretical concepts related to the study of culture.
51 Phys34F, conducted 04/29/10.
52 See Abbott, *The System of Professions.*
53 See Mather, McEwen, and Maiman, *Divorce Lawyers at Work.*
54 See Allen, "The Nursing-Medical Boundary," 498–520; Reverby, *Ordered to Care*; and Rosenberg, *The Care of Strangers.*
55 See Shuval, "Nurses in Alternative Health Care," 1784–95. See also Shuval and Nissim, "Changing Boundaries," 675–90.
56 Phys52F, conducted 10/28/10.

APPENDIX A

1 National Research Council, *Research-Doctorate Programs.*
2 Preston, *Leaving Science.*
3 Van Anders, "Why the Academic Pipeline Leaks."
4 Ladd and Lipset, *The Divided Academy.*
5 Davies and Harre, "Positioning," 43–63.
6 Thomas and Thomas, *The Child in America.*
7 Bourdieu, *Language and Symbolic Power.*

REFERENCES

Abbott, Andrew. *The System of Professions*. Chicago: University of Chicago Press, 1988.

Acker, Joan. "Hierarchies, Jobs, and Bodies: A Theory of Gendered Organizations." *Gender and Society* 4, no. 2 (June 1990): 139–58.

Allen, Davina. "The Nursing-Medical Boundary: A Negotiated Order?" *Sociology of Health and Illness* 19, no. 4 (September 1997): 498–520.

Anderson, Nick. "American University Professor Breast-Feeds Sick Baby in Class, Sparking Debate." *Washington Post*, September 11, 2012. http://www.washington-post.com/local/education/american-university-professor-breast-feeds-sick-baby-in-class-sparking-debate/2012/09/11/54a06856-fc12-11e1-8adc-499661afe377_story.html.

Artis, Julie. "Breastfeed at Your Own Risk." *Contexts* 8, no. 4 (November 2009): 28–34.

Astone, Nan Marie, Jacinda K. Dariotis, Freya L. Sonenstein, Joseph H. Pleck, and Kathryn Hynes. "Men's Work Efforts and the Transition to Fatherhood." *Journal of Family and Economic Issues* 31, no. 1 (March 2010): 3–13.

Aumann, Kerstin, Ellen Galinsky, and Kenneth Matos. *The New Male Mystique*. New York: Families and Work Institute, 2011.

Baer, Michael, and Claire Van Ummersen. *An Agenda for Excellence: Creating Flexibility in Tenure-Track Faculty Careers*. Washington, DC: American Council on Education, 2005.

Bardin, Jon. "For Science Ph.D.'s, There Is No One True Path." *Chronicle of Higher Education*, March 25, 2012. http://chronicle.com/article/For-Science-PhDs-There Is/131307/?sid=at&utm_source=at&utm_medium=en.

Becher, Tony, and Paul Trowler. *Academic Tribes and Territories: Intellectual Enquiry and the Cultures of Discipline*. Philadelphia, PA: Open University Press, 2001.

Becker, Gary S. *Treatise on the Family*. Cambridge, MA: Harvard University Press, 1981.

Bernstein, Rachel. "No Sexism in Science? Not So Fast, Critics Say." *Science* 346, no. 6211 (November 2014): 798.

Bianchi, Suzanne M., John P. Robinson, and Melissa A. Milkie. *Changing Rhythms of American Family Life*. New York: Russell Sage Foundation, 2006.

Bielby, Denise Del Vento, and William T. Bielby. "Work Commitment, Sex Role Attitudes, and Women's Employment." *American Sociological Review* 49, no. 2 (April 1984): 234–47.

Blair-Loy, Mary. *Competing Devotions: Career and Family among Women Executives*. Cambridge, MA: Harvard University Press, 2003.

Blalock, Hubert M., Jr. *Toward a Theory of Minority-Group Relations*. New York: Wiley, 1967.

Blau, Judith. "Expertise and Power in Professional Organization." *Sociology of Work and Occupations* 6, no. 1 (1979): 102–23.

Bourdieu, Pierre. *Language and Symbolic Power*. Cambridge, MA: Harvard University Press, 1991.

Bureau of Labor Statistics. "Table 2: Employment Status of the Civilian Non-institutional Population 16 Years and over by Sex, 1970–2010 Annual Averages." http://www.bls.gov/cps/wlf-table2-2011.pdf.

———. "Table 24. Contribution of Wives' Earnings to Family Income, 1970–2009." http://www.bls.gov/cps/wlf-table24-2011.pdf.

———. "Table 25. Wives Who Earn More Than Their Husbands, 1987–2009." http://www.bls.gov/cps/wlf-table25-2011.pdf.

Cech, Erin, Brian Rubineaub, Susan Silbey, and Caroll Serond. "Professional Role Confidence and Gendered Persistence in Engineering." *American Sociological Review* 765, no. 5 (October 2011): 641–66.

Ceci, Stephen J., Wendy M. Williams, and Susan M. Barnett. "Women's Underrepresentation in Science: Sociocultural and Biological Considerations." *Psychological Bulletin* 135, no. 2 (March 2009): 218–61.

Cha, Youngjoo. "Reinforcing Separate Spheres." *American Sociological Review* 75, no. 2 (April 2010): 303–29.

"The Child Care Tuition Assistance Program (CCTAP) for UW-Madison Students." University of Wisconsin–Madison. February 6, 2013. http://www.occfr.wisc.edu/cctapinfo.htm.

Cole, Jonathan R., and Harriet Zuckerman. "Marriage, Motherhood and Research Performance in Science." *Scientific American* 256, no. 2 (February 1987): 119–25.

Coltrane, Scott. "Elite Careers and Family Commitment: It's (Still) about Gender." *Annals of the American Academy of Political and Social Sciences* 596 (November 2004): 214–20.

Coontz, Stephanie. *The Way We Never Were: American Families and the Nostalgia Trap*. New York: Basic Books, 1992.

Cooper, Marianne. "Being the 'Go-to Guy': Fatherhood, Masculinity, and the Organization of Work in Silicon Valley." *Qualitative Sociology* 23, no. 4 (December 2000): 379–405.

Correll, Shelley. "Constraints into Preferences: Gender, Status and Emerging Career Aspirations." *American Sociological Review* 69, no. 1 (February 2004): 93–113.

———. "Gender and the Career Choice Process: The Role of Biased Self-Assessments." *American Journal of Sociology* 106, no. 6 (May 2001): 1691–730.

Correll, Shelley, Stephen Benard, and In Paik. "Getting a Job: Is There a Motherhood Penalty?" *American Journal Sociology* 112, no. 5 (March 2007): 1297–338.

Coser, Lewis A. *Greedy Institutions: Patterns of Undivided Commitment*. New York: Free Press, 1974.

Cyranoski, David, Natasha Gilbert, Heidi Ledford, Anjali Nayar, and Mohammed Yahia. "Education: The PhD Factory." *Nature* 472 (April 2011): 276–79.

Damaske, Sarah, Elaine Howard Ecklund, Anne Lincoln, and Virginia White. "Male Scientists' Competing Devotions to Work and Family: Changing Norms in a Male-Dominated Profession." *Work and Occupations* 41, no. 4 (November 2012): 477–507.

Damaske, Sarah, and Kathleen Gerson. "Viewing 21st Century Motherhood through a Work-Family Lens." In *The Handbook of Work-Family Integration: Research, Theory and Best Practices*, ed. Karen Korabik, Donna S. Lero, and Denise S. Whitehead, 233–48. Oxford: Academic Press, 2008.

Davies, Bronwyn, and Rom Harre. "Positioning: The Discursive Production of Selves." *Journal for the Theory of Social Behavior* 20, no. 1 (March 1990): 43–63.

Demos, Vasilikie, Catherine White Berheide, and Marcia Texler Segal, eds. *Advances in Gender Research*. Bingley, UK: Emerald Group, 2014.

Didion, Catherine Jay. "Dual Careers and Shared Positions: Adjusting University Policy to Accommodate Academic Couples." *Journal of College Science Teaching* 26, no. 2 (November 1996): 123–24.

DiMaggio, Paul. "Culture and Cognition." *Annual Review of Sociology* 23 (August 1997): 263–87.

DiMaggio, Paul, and Walter W. Powell. "The Iron Cage Revisited: Institutional Isomorphism and Collective Rationality in Organizational Fields." *American Sociological Review* 48, no. 2 (April 1983): 147–60.

Douglas, Mary. *How Institutions Think*. Syracuse, NY: Syracuse University Press, 1986.

Drago, Robert, Ann C. Crouter, Mark Wardell, and Billie S. Willits. "Faculty and Families Project: The Pennsylvania State University—The Final Report to the Sloan Foundation." Work-Family Working Paper 01-02 for the Faculty and Families Project, Department of Labor Studies and Industrial Relations, Penn State University, University Park, PA, 2001.

Ducharme, Lori J., and Jack K. Martin. "Unrewarding Work, Coworker Support, and Job Satisfaction." *Work and Occupations* 27, no. 2 (May 2000): 223–43.

Dye, Thomas R. *Top Down Policymaking*. New York: Chatham House, 2001.

Ecklund, Elaine Howard, and Anne E. Lincoln. "Scientists Want More Children." *PLoS ONE* 6, no. 8 (August 2011): e22590.

Ecklund, Elaine Howard, Anne Lincoln, and Cassandra Tansey. "Gender Segregation in Elite Academic Science." *Gender and Society* 26, no. 5 (October 2012): 693–717.

Ecklund, Elaine Howard, and Elizabeth Long. "Spirituality and Science." *Sociology of Religion* 72, no. 3 (February 2011): 253–74.

Edgell, Penny. *Religion and Family in a Changing Society*. Princeton, NJ: Princeton University Press, 2006.

Edin, Kathryn, and Timothy J. Nelson. *Doing the Best I Can: Fatherhood in the Inner City*. Berkeley: University of California Press, 2013.

England, Paula. *Comparable Worth: Theories and Evidence*. New York: Aldine Transaction, 1992.

England, Paula, Paul Allison, Su Li, Noah Mark, Jennifer Thompson, Michelle Budig, and Han Sun. "Why Are Some Academic Fields Tipping toward Female? The Sex Composition of U.S. Fields of Doctoral Degree Receipt, 1971–2002." *Sociology of Education* 80, no. 1 (January 2007): 23–42.

Epstein, Cynthia Fuchs, Carroll Seron, Bonnie Oglensky, and Robert Sauté. *The Part-Time Paradox: Time Norms, Professional Life, Family and Gender*. New York: Routledge, 1999.

"Fathers/Program Helps Dads Deal with Stress." *Milwaukee Journal Sentinel*, June 12, 1996. http://news.google.com/newspapers?nid=1683&dat=19960612&id=3EscAAAAIBAJ&sjid=BS4EAAAAIBAJ&pg=6866,2218332.

Ferber, Marianne, and Jane Loeb, eds. *Academic Couples: Problems and Promises*. Champaign: University of Illinois Press, 1997.

Folbre, Nancy. *The Invisible Heart: Economics and Family Values*. New York: New Press, 2002.

———. *Valuing Children: Rethinking the Economics of Family*. Cambridge, MA: Harvard University Press, 2007.

Fox, Mary Frank. "Gender, Family Characteristics, and Publication Productivity among Scientists." *Social Studies of Science* 35, no. 1 (February 2005): 131–50.

———. "Women and Men Faculty in Academic Science and Engineering: Social-Organizational Indicators and Implications." *American Behavioral Scientist* 53, no. 7 (March 2010): 997–1012.

———. "Women and Scientific Careers." In *Handbook of Science and Technology Studies*, ed. Sheila Jasanoff, Gerald E. Markle, James C. Petersen, and Trevor Pinch, 205–24. New York: Sage, 1995.

———. "Women, Science, and Academia: Graduate Education and Careers." *Gender and Society* 15, no. 5 (October 2001): 654–66.

Fox, Mary Frank, Carolyn Fonseca, and Jinghui Bao. "Work and Family Conflict in Academic Science: Patterns and Predictors among Women and Men in Research Universities." *Social Studies of Science* 41, no. 5 (October 2011): 715–35.

Frehill, Lisa M. "Education and Occupational Sex Segregation: The Decision to Major in Engineering." *Sociological Quarterly* 38, no. 2 (March 1997): 225–49.

Gauchat, Gordon. "Politicization of Science in the Public Sphere: A Study of Public Trust in the United States." *American Sociological Review* 77, no. 2 (April 2012): 167–87.

Geiger, Roger L. *To Advance Knowledge: The Growth of American Research Universities, 1900–1940*. New York: Oxford University Press, 1986.

Gerson, Kathleen. *No Man's Land: Men's Changing Commitments to Family and Work*. New York: Basic Books, 1993.

———. *The Unfinished Revolution: How a New Generation Is Reshaping Family, Work, and Gender in America*. New York: Oxford University Press, 2010.

Gibbons, Michael, Peter Scott, Helga Nowotny, Camille Limoges, Martin Trow, and Simon Schwartzman. *The New Production of Knowledge: The Dynamics of Science and Research in Contemporary Societies*. London: Sage, 1994.

Gieryn, Thomas F. "Boundary-Work and the Demarcation of Science from Non-science: Strains and Interests in Professional Ideologies of Scientists." *American Sociological Review* 48, no. 6 (December 1983): 781–95.
Glass, Jennifer L., and Sarah Beth Estes. "The Family Responsive Workplace." *Annual Review of Sociology* 23 (August 1997): 289–313.
Glauber, Rebecca. 2008. "Gender and Race in Families and at Work: The Fatherhood Wage Premium." *Gender and Society* 22, no. 1 (February 2008): 8–30.
Glick, Peter, Korin Wilk, and Michele Perreault. "Images of Occupations: Components of Gender and Status in Occupational Stereotypes." *Sex Roles* 32, no. 9–10 (May 1995): 565–82.
Gornick, Janet C., and Marcia Meyers. *Families That Work: Policies for Reconciling Parenthood and Employment*. New York : Russell Sage Foundation, 2003.
Greenwood, Davydd, and Morten Levin. "Re-organizing Universities and 'Knowing How': University Restructuring and Knowledge Creation for the 21st Century." *Organization* 8, no. 2 (May 2001): 433–40.
Hakim, Catherine. "Lifestyle Preferences as Determinants of Women's Differentiated Labour Market Careers." *Work and Occupations* 29, no. 4 (November 2002): 428–59.
Harrington, Brad. *Career Management and Work-Life Integration: Using Self-Assessment to Navigate Contemporary Careers*. Thousand Oaks, CA: Sage, 2007.
Harvard University. "Child Care." February 6, 2013. http://childcare.harvard.edu/.
Hays, Sharon. *The Cultural Contradictions of Motherhood*. New Haven, CT: Yale University Press, 1996.
Hermanowicz, Joseph C. *Lives in Science: How Institutions Affect Academic Careers*. Chicago: University of Chicago Press, 2009.
———. *The Stars Are Not Enough: Scientists—Their Passions and Professions*. Chicago: University of Chicago Press, 1998.
Hill, E. Jeffrey, Chongming Yang, Alan J. Hawkins, and Maria Ferris. "A Cross-Cultural Test of the Work-Family Interface in 48 Countries." *Journal of Marriage and Family* 66, no. 5 (December 2004): 1300–1316.
Hirschman, Albert O. *Exit, Voice, and Loyalty: Responses to Decline in Firms, Organizations, and States*. Cambridge, MA: Harvard University Press, 1970.
Hochschild, Arlie R. *The Managed Heart: Commercialization of Human Feeling*. Berkeley: University of California Press, 1985.
———. *The Time Bind: When Work Becomes Home and Home Becomes Work*. New York: Metropolitan Books, 1997.
Hochschild, Arlie R., and Anne Machung. *The Second Shift: Working Parents and the Revolution at Home*. New York: Viking Penguin, 1989.
Jacobs, Jerry A., and Kathleen Gerson. 2004. *The Time Divide: Work, Family, and Gender Inequality*. Cambridge, MA: Harvard University Press, 2004.
Jacobs, Jerry A., and Sarah E. Winslow. "Overworked Faculty: Job Stresses and Family Demands." *Annals of the American Academy of Political and Social Science* 596, no. 1 (November 2004): 104–29.

Johnson, David R., Elaine Howard Ecklund, and Anne E. Lincoln. "Narratives of Science Outreach in Elite Contexts of Academic Science." *Science Communication* 36, no. 1 (February 2014): 81–105.

Kanter, Rosabeth Moss. *Men and Women of the Corporation*. New York: Basic Books, 1997.

Keene, Jennifer Reid, and Jill Quadagno. "Predictors of Perceived Work-Family Balance: Gender Difference or Gender Similarity?" *Sociological Perspectives* 47, no. 1 (March 2004): 1–23.

Keller, Evelyn Fox. "The Origin, History, and Politics of the Subject Called 'Gender and Science': A First Person Account." In *Handbook of Science and Technology Studies*, ed. Sheila Jasanoff, Gerald E. Markle, James C. Petersen, and Trevor Pinch, 80–94. New York: Sage, 1995.

Kelly, Alison. "The Construction of Masculine Science." *British Journal of Sociology of Education* 6, no. 2 (1985): 133–54.

Kelly, Erin L., Samantha K. Ammons, Kelly Chermack, and Phyllis Moen. "Gendered Challenge, Gendered Response Confronting the Ideal Worker Norm in a White-Collar Organization." *Gender and Society* 24, no. 3 (June 2010): 281–303.

Kerber, Linda K. "We Must Make the Academic Workplace More Humane and Equitable." *Chronicle of Higher Education*, March 18, 2005, B6–B9.

Ladd, Everett Carll, Jr., and Seymour Martin Lipset. *The Divided Academy: Professors and Politics*. New York: McGraw-Hill, 1975.

Lamont, Michèle. *Money, Morals, and Manners: The Culture of the French and American Upper-Middle Class*. Chicago: University of Chicago Press, 1992.

Latour, Bruno, and Steve Woolgar. *Laboratory Life: The Construction of Scientific Facts*. Beverly Hills, CA: Sage, 1979.

Leslie, Sarah-Jane, Andrei Cimplian, Meredith Meyer, and Edward Freeland. "Expectations of Brilliance Underlie Gender Distributions across Academic Disciplines." *Science* 347, no. 6219 (January 2015): 262–65.

Lindsay, Michael. *Faith in the Halls of Power*. New York: Oxford University Press, 2007.

Lingston, Gretchen, and D'Vera Cohn. "Childlessness Up among All Women; Down among Women with Advanced Degrees." *Pew Research Social and Demographic Trends*. June 25, 2010. http://www.pewsocialtrends.org/2010/06/25/childlessness-up-among-all-women-down-among-women-with-advanced-degrees/.

Long, Elizabeth. "Stories as Carriers of Theory." Paper presented at the Culture Section MiniConference, annual meeting of the American Sociological Association, New York, August 15, 2007.

Long, J. Scott. "Discussion: Problems and Prospects for Research on Sex Differences." In *Women: Their Underrepresentation and Career Differentials in Science and Engineering*, ed. Linda S. Dix, 157–69. Washington, DC: National Research Council, 1987.

Long, Paul Leslie. "The Aesthetics of Class in Post-war Britain." PhD diss., University of Warwick, 2001.

Lundberg, Shelly, and Elaina Rose. "Parenthood and the Earnings of Married Men and Women." *Labour Economics* 7, no. 6 (2000): 689–710.

Maldonado, Theresa, and Anita La Salle. "Dear Colleague Letter: Career-Life Balance (CLB) Initiative." National Science Foundation. 2011. http://www.nsf.gov/pubs/2012/nsf12065/nsf12065.pdf.

Martinez, Gladys M., Anjani Chandra, Joyce C. Abma, Jo Jones, and William D. Mosher. "Fertility, Contraception, and Fatherhood: Data on Men and Women from Cycle 6 (2002) of the National Survey of Family Growth." *Vital and Health Statistics* 23, no. 26 (May 2006): 1–142.

Mason, Mary Ann, and Marc Goulden. "Do Babies Matter (Part II)? Closing the Baby Gap." *Academe* 90, no. 6 (November–December 2004): 1–10.

———. "Marriage and Baby Blues: Redefining Gender Equity in the Academy." *Annals of the American Academy of Political and Social Science* 596, no. 1 (November 2004): 86–103.

Mason, Mary Ann, Marc Goulden, and Karie Frasch. "Keeping Women in the Science Pipeline." Presentation at the conference "Focus on Workplace Flexibility," Alfred P. Sloan Foundation, Georgetown University, Washington, DC, November 29–30, 2010.

Mason, Mary Ann, Nicholas H. Wolfinger, and Marc Goulden. *Do Babies Matter? Gender and Family in the Ivory Tower*. New Brunswick, NJ: Rutgers University Press, 2013.

Mather, Lynn, Craig A. McEwen, and Richard J. Maiman. *Divorce Lawyers at Work: Varieties of Professionalism in Practice*. New York: Oxford University Press, 2001.

Maume, David J. "Gender Differences in Restricting Work Efforts Because of Family Responsibilities." *Journal of Marriage and Family* 68, no. 4 (November 2006): 859–69.

McDonnell, Fiona. "Why So Few Choose Physics: An Alternative Explanation for the Leaky Pipeline." *American Journal of Physics* 73, no. 7 (July 2005): 583–86.

Mennino, Sue Falter, and April Brayfield. "Job-Family Trade-offs: The Multidimensional Effect of Gender." *Work and Occupations* 29, no. 2 (May 2002): 226–56.

Milkie, Melissa A., Marybeth J. Mattingly, Kei M. Nomaguchi, Suzanne M. Bianchi, and John P. Robinson. "The Time Squeeze: Parental Statuses and Feelings about Time with Children." *Journal of Marriage and Family* 66, no. 3 (August 2004): 739–61.

Misra, Joya, Jennifer Hickes Lundquist, and Abby Templer. "Gender, Work Time, and Care Responsibilities among Faculty." *Sociological Forum* 27, no. 2 (June 2012): 300–323.

Moen, Phyllis. *Women's Two Roles: A Contemporary Dilemma*. Westport, CT: Greenwood, 1992.

Moen, Phyllis, and Patricia Roehling. *The Career Mystique: Cracks in the American Dream*. Lanham, MD: Rowman and Littlefield, 2005.

Moen, Phyllis, and Yan Yu. "Effective Work/Life Strategies: Working Couples, Work Conditions, Gender, and Life Quality." *Social Problems* 47, no. 3 (August 2000): 291–326.

National Academy of Sciences, National Academy of Engineering, and Institute of Medicine of the National Academies. *Beyond Bias and Barriers: Fulfilling the Potential of Women in Academic Science and Engineering*. Washington, DC: National Academy Press, 2006.

National Institutes of Health. "Research Project Grants: Competing Applications, Awards, Success Rate and Total Funding." 2013. http://report.nih.gov/FileLink.aspx?rid=565.

National Research Council. *Research-Doctorate Programs in the United States: Continuity and Change*. 1995. http://www.nap.edu/readingroom/books/researchdoc/.

National Science Foundation. "Graduate Enrollment in S&E Fields, by Enrollment Status, Sex, Citizenship, and Race/Ethnicity, and in Health Fields: 1999–2008." 2010. http://www.nsf.gov/statistics/infbrief/nsf10320/tab1.xls.

———. "US NSF—Frequently Asked Questions Related to Dependent Care—nsf10032." 2013. http://www.nsf.gov/pubs/policydocs/clb/clbfaqs.jsp#1.

Nerad, Maresi, and Joseph Cerny. "Postdoctoral Patterns, Career Advancement, and Problems." *Science* 285, no. 5433 (September 1999): 1533–35.

Nippert-Eng, Christena. *Home and Work: Negotiating Boundaries through Everyday Life*. Chicago: University of Chicago Press, 2008.

Orit, Avishai. "Five Myths about Breast-feeding." *Washington Post Opinions*, May 31, 2012. http://www.washingtonpost.com/opinions/five-myths-about-breast-feeding/2012/05/31/gJQAt6774U_story.html.

Owens, Jennifer, Krista Carothers, Kristen Willoughby, Michele Siegel, and Kaisa Filppula. "Data from the 2012 Working Mother 100 Best Companies." *Working Mother*, September 13, 2012. http://www.workingmother.com/best-companies/data-2012-working-mother-100-best-companies.

Parker, Kim, and Wendy Wang. "Modern Parenthood: Role of Moms and Dads Converge as They Balance Work and Family." *Pew Research Center's Social and Demographic Trends Project*. March 14, 2013. http://www.pewsocialtrends.org/2013/03/14/modern-parenthood-roles-of-moms-and-dads-converge-as-they-balance-work-and-family/.

Patten, Eileen, and Kim Parker. "A Gender Reversal on Career Aspirations: Young Women Now Top Young Men in Valuing a High-Paying Career." *Pew Research Social and Demographic Trends*. April 19, 2012. http://www.pewsocialtrends.org/2012/04/19/a-gender-reversal-on-career-aspirations/.

Polachek, Solomon. "How the Life-Cycle Human Capital Model Explains Why the Gender Wage Gap Narrowed." In *The Declining Significance of Gender?*, ed. Francine D. Blau, Mary C. Brinton, and David Grusky, 102–24. New York: Russell Sage Foundation, 2006.

Preston, Anne E. *Leaving Science: Occupational Exit from Scientific Careers*. New York: Russell Sage Foundation, 2004.

———. "Plugging the Leaks in the Scientific Workforce." *Issues in Science and Technology* 20, no. 4 (Summer 2004): 69–74.

Reverby, Susan M. *Ordered to Care: The Dilemma of American Nursing, 1850–1945*. Cambridge: Cambridge University Press, 1987.

Rippeyoung, Phyllis, and Mary C. Noonan. "Is Breastfeeding Truly Cost Free? Income Consequences of Breastfeeding for Women." *American Sociological Review* 77, no. 2 (April 2012): 244–67.
Risman, Barbara. *Families as They Really Are*. New York: Norton, 2009.
Rosenberg, Charles E. *The Care of Strangers: The Rise of America's Hospital System*. New York: Basic Books, 1987.
Rosser, Sue V., and Mark Zachary Taylor. "Why Are We Still Worried about Women in Science?" *Academe* 95, no. 3 (May–June 2009): 7–10.
Sagan, Carl. *Cosmos*. New York: Ballantine Books, 1985.
Schiebinger, Londa, Andrea Davies Henderson, and Shannon Gilmartin. *Dual-Career Academic Couples: What Universities Need to Know*. Stanford, CA: Michelle R. Clayman Institute for Gender Study, Stanford University, 2008.
Schieman, Scott, and Paul Glavin. "Trouble at the Border? Gender, Flexibility at Work, and the Work-Home Interface." *Social Problems* 55, no. 4 (November 2008): 590–611.
Schieman, Scott, Melissa A. Milkie, and Paul Glavin. "When Work Interferes with Life: Work-Nonwork Interference and the Interference of Work-Related Demands and Resources." *American Sociological Review* 74, no. 6 (December 2009): 966–88.
Schmander, Toni. "Gender Identification Moderates Stereotype Threat Effects on Women's Math Performance." *Journal of Experimental Social Psychology* 38, no. 2 (March 2002): 194–201.
Shapin, Steven. *The Scientific Life: A Moral History of a Late Modern Vocation*. Chicago: University of Chicago Press, 2008.
Shauman, Kimberlee A., and Yu Xie. "Geographic Mobility of Scientists: Sex Differences and Family Constraints." *Demography* 33, no. 4 (November 1996): 455–68.
Shepherd, Linda Jean. *Lifting the Veil: The Feminine Face of Science*. Boston: Shambhala, 1993.
Shuval, Judith. "Nurses in Alternative Health Care: Integrating Medical Paradigms." *Social Science and Medicine* 63, no. 7 (October 2006): 1784–95.
Shuval, Judith T., and Mizrachi Nissim. "Changing Boundaries: Modes of Coexistence of Alternative and Biomedicine." *Qualitative Health Research* 14, no. 5 (May 2004): 675–90.
Smith-Doerr, Laurel. *Women's Work: Gender Equity v. Hierarchy in the Life Sciences*. Boulder, CO: Lynne Rienner, 2004.
"Statement of the American Sociological Association Council on the Causes of Gender Differences in Science and Math Career Achievement: Harvard's Lawrence Summers and the Ensuing Public Debate." February 28, 2005. http://www2.asanet.org/public/summers.html.
Stewart, Abigail J., Janet E. McMalley, and Danielle LaVaque-Manty, eds. *Transforming Science and Engineering: Advancing Academic Women*. Ann Arbor: University of Michigan Press, 2007.
"Supply Side Academics." *Nature Neuroscience* 10, no. 11 (November 2007): 1337.

Taylor, Catherine. "Occupational Sex Composition and the Gendered Availability of Workplace Support." *Gender and Society* 24, no. 2 (April 2010): 189–212.

Thomas, William Isaac, and Dorothy Swaine Thomas. *The Child in America: Behavior Problems and Programs*. New York: Knopf, 1928.

Trow, Martin. *Technical Report: Carnegie Commission National Survey of Higher Education*. Carnegie Commission on Higher Education. June 1972.

"United States." CIA World Fact Book. https://www.cia.gov/library/publications/the-world-factbook/fields/2102.html.

U.S. Department of Health and Human Services, Office on Women's Health. "HHS Blueprint for Action on Breastfeeding." 2000. https://www.womenshealth.gov/archive/breastfeeding/programs/blueprints/bluprntbk2.pdf.

Van Anders, Sari M. "Why the Academic Pipeline Leaks: Fewer Men Than Women Perceive Barriers to Becoming Professors?" *Sex Roles* 51, nos. 9/10 (November 2004): 511–21.

Wall, Glenda, and Stephanie Arnold. "How Involved Is Involved Fathering?" *Gender and Society* 21, no. 4 (August 2007): 508–27.

Weber, Max. *The Methodology of the Social Sciences*. New York: Simon and Schuster, 1949.

Whittington, Kjersten Bunker, and Laurel Smith-Doerr. "Women Inventors in Context: Disparities in Patenting across Academia and Industry." *Gender and Society* 22, no. 2 (April 2008): 194–218.

Whyte, William H. *The Organization Man*. New York: Simon and Schuster, 1956.

Williams, Christine. *Gender Differences at Work: Women and Men in Nontraditional Occupations*. Berkeley: University of California Press, 1989.

———. *Still a Man's World: Men Who Do "Women's Work."* Berkeley: University of California Press, 1995.

Williams, Joan. *Reshaping the Work-Family Debate: Why Men and Class Matter*. Cambridge, MA: Harvard University Press, 2010.

———. *Unbending Gender: Why Family and Work Conflict and What to Do about It*. New York: Oxford University Press, 2000.

Williams, Joan, and Heather Boushey. "The Three Faces of Work-Family Conflict: The Poor, the Professionals, and the Missing Middle." Center for American Progress. January 25, 2010. https://www.americanprogress.org/issues/labor/report/2010/01/25/7194/the-three-faces-of-work-family-conflict/.

Wolfinger, Nicholas H., Mary Ann Mason, and Marc Goulden. "Problems in the Pipeline: Gender, Marriage, and Fertility in the Ivory Tower." *Journal of Higher Education* 79, no. 4 (July 2008): 388–405.

Wolf-Wendel, Lisa E., Susan Twombly, and Suzanne Rice. "Dual Career Couples: Keeping Them Together." *Journal of Higher Education* 71, no. 3 (May–June 2000): 291–321.

World Bank. "Fertility Rate, Total (Births per Woman)." December 22, 2015. http://data.worldbank.org/indicator/SP.DYN.TFRT.IN.

Wuthnow, Robert. *Meaning and Moral Order: Explorations in Cultural Analysis*. Berkeley: University of California Press, 1987.

Xie, Yu, and Kimberlee A. Shauman. *Women in Science: Career Processes and Outcomes*. Cambridge, MA: Harvard University Press, 2003.
Zimmermann, Karin. "Gender Knowledge under Construction: The Case of the European Union's Science and Research Policy." In *Gender Change in Academia: Re-mapping the Fields of Work, Knowledge, and Politics from a Gender Perspective*, ed. Birgit Riegraf, Brigitte Aulenbacher, Edit Kirsch-Auwärter, and Ursula Müller. 173–87. Wiesbaden: VS Verlag für Sozialwissenschaften, 2010.
Zuckerman, Harriet. "Stratification in American Science." *Sociological Inquiry* 40, no. 2 (April 1970): 235–57.
Zuckerman, Harriet, Jonathan Cole, and John Bruer. *The Outer Circle: Women in the Scientific Community*. New York: Norton, 1991.
Zuo, Jiping. "The Effect of Men's Breadwinner Status on Their Changing Gender Beliefs." *Sex Roles* 37, nos. 9/10 (November 1997): 799–816.

INDEX

ABOUT THE AUTHORS

Elaine Howard Ecklund is the Herbert S. Autrey Chair in Social Sciences at Rice University, where she is also founding Director of the Religion and Public Life Program and Rice Scholar at the Baker Institute for Public Policy. She is the author of *Korean American Evangelicals: New Models for Civic Life* and *Science vs. Religion: What Scientists Really Think*.

Anne E. Lincoln is Associate Professor of Sociology at Southern Methodist University.